THE CHANDRA LEVY CASE

50 States of Crime:

NEW YORK: THE ALICE CRIMMINS CASE

CALIFORNIA: THE GOLDEN STATE KILLER CASE

OHIO: THE CLEVELAND JOHN DOE CASE

MISSISSIPPI: THE EMMETT TILL CASE

SOUTH CAROLINA: THE MURDAUGH MURDERS CASE

WASHINGTON, DC: THE CHANDRA LEVY CASE

 **WASHINGTON, DC**

THE CHANDRA LEVY CASE

HÉLÈNE COUTARD
TRANSLATED BY LAURIE BENNETT

CRIME INK
CRIME INK
NEW YORK

THE CHANDRA LEVY CASE

Crime Ink
An Imprint of Penzler Publishers
58 Warren Street
New York, N.Y. 10007

© Editions 10/18, Département d'Univers Poche, 2024
In association with So Press/Society
English translation copyright: © 2025 by Laurie Bennett

First edition

Cover design by Charles Perry, inspired by the French language edition cover design by Nicolas Caminade

Interior design by Maria Fernandez

All rights reserved. No part of this book may be reproduced in whole or in part without written permission from the publisher, except by reviewers who may quote brief excerpts in connection with a review in a newspaper, magazine, or electronic publication; nor may any part of this book be reproduced, stored in a retrieval system, or transmitted in any form or by any means electronic, mechanical, photocopying, recording, or other, or used to train generative artificial intelligence (AI) technologies, without written permission from the publisher.

Library of Congress Control Number: 2025935478

Paperback ISBN: 978-1-61316-696-3
eBook ISBN: 978-1-61316-697-0

10 9 8 7 6 5 4 3 2 1

Printed in the United States of America

Contents

Prologue	1
THE WOMAN WHO VANISHED FROM DUPONT CIRCLE	15
1. Seven Months in DC	17
2. Chandra Drama	44
3. Condit Country	64
ROCK CREEK PARK	83
1. The World After 9/11	85
2. Parallel Investigations	98
3. Unanswered Questions	106
THE MAN IN THE PARK	115
1. Who Killed Chandra Levy?	117
2. Conflicting Stories	126
3. House of Cards	143
JUSTICE FOR CHANDRA	149
1. The Cover-up	151
2. The Horse Whisperer	165
3. Serial Killer	172

Epilogue	183
APPENDICES	193
Rock Creek Park	195
Downtown Washington	197
Timeline	199
Sources	203
Acknowledgments	205

PROLOGUE

The United Airlines flight from San Francisco to Washington takes five hours and eleven minutes. On September 14, 2000, Chandra Levy had five hours and eleven minutes to think about what she was leaving behind and what she hoped to find at the other end of the country. She was twenty-three, and her life was just beginning. From high up in the sky, Chandra watched California fading away through the window. She couldn't make out her hometown, Modesto, ninety miles inland from San Francisco. But that was OK; she'd already seen enough of Modesto.

For eighteen years, she had roamed Modesto's wide, straight, predictable streets—streets that belonged more in a Midwestern town than a California city. For eighteen years, she had watched truck after truck drive by, passing one Starbucks after another. With a population of 180,000 and fair weather year-round, Modesto had inspired only two things throughout its history: George Lucas's *American Graffiti* and a yearning to leave, felt by every young person like Chandra.

Chenault Drive, the street she'd grown up on, was one of the nicest parts of town. A line of sprawling ranch houses stretched all the way down the long cul-de-sac, each backing onto wide, open yards. The Levys had a big pool and even owned horses, although Chandra didn't care for them much. They were her mom's darlings.

Chandra preferred to read books, run her fingers up and down the keys of the family's big, glossy piano, and gaze up at the stars through her telescope. She loved the *Star Wars* movies, baseball stats, the San Francisco Giants, Reese's peanut butter cups, and Harrison Ford. When it came to pets, she opted for birds over horses and had four of them: Franny and Zooey, like the J. D. Salinger characters, and Christmas and Hanukkah, for the blend of spiritual beliefs she'd been raised with.

Although Modesto as a whole was unremarkable, the downtown area was dotted with small art galleries, a few retro cinemas, and shops selling little Buddha sculptures and colorful gemstones. Susan Levy, Chandra's mother, was an artist, so maybe it was this cultural and spiritual side of the town that had quickly won her over.

Though Chandra was now flying more than twenty-five hundred miles away from her parents—determined to build a life for herself—the thought of Bob and Susan always made her smile. There was something a little wacky about her parents. For starters, they had named her Chandra, which is Sanskrit for "girl above the moon and stars." Her father, Bob, was an oncologist known for his holistic approach to cancer treatments. Around town, people called him "Last Chance Bob."

He and Chandra were quite close. In his eyes, she could do no wrong. Chandra was his princess, his little ladybug . . . and Chandra had no problem being a daddy's girl. In her world, Bob was a rock and the person who could never say "no" to her, which was just as well because Chandra did not take kindly to being told what to do. As for free-spirited Susan, Chandra affectionately called her "Looney Susan."

Why the Levys ended up in Modesto in the first place was pure luck of the draw. Quite literally. When Chandra, their first child, was born in 1977, Bob had just finished his residency in Ohio and the couple was looking to move. They made a shortlist of cities in dire need of an oncologist, scribbled each name onto a strip of paper, then dropped them all into a baseball cap and drew one at random. The family could just as well have ended up in Las Cruces, New Mexico, or Council Bluffs, Iowa, but on that day in 1977, they pulled Modesto, California, from the cap.

The day before her flight, Chandra had packed her suitcase. In her room on the second floor, she paused and took in the space around her. As always, the top of her rattan dresser was buried under an overflowing jewelry box and a chaotic pile of beauty products. Her gaze lingered on the beige-and-white walls covered in keepsakes: her ticket stub from the 1989 World Series game she'd attended with her dad—the Giants had lost to the Oakland Athletics, but nothing could tarnish her memory of that day, not the defeat nor the earthquake that delayed the start of the game—her high school and San Francisco State University diplomas, a copy of *Men Are from Mars, Women Are from Venus*, and souvenirs from family trips to France, Israel, Tanzania, and Costa Rica.

As the plane flew over the Sierra Nevada, each peak shrouded in cloud, Chandra reflected on her high school

PROLOGUE

years. It would be a lie to say that she was the coolest kid in school. In ninth grade, she wore a retainer and struggled to fit in. It didn't help that she came down with mononucleosis and missed five weeks of class without even kissing a boy. In class, she was understimulated and struggled to keep her grades up.

Then one day, something just clicked: School wasn't going to last forever. What if she was destined for a more exciting future than what this small-town high school had to offer? Maybe she'd be better off opting out of the school cliques and their social codes, all the impossible expectations of teens in the nineties, to instead prepare for that future right now? And that's exactly what she did.

You have to picture it. At just five foot three, Chandra was a small thing with a mess of unruly curls, pushing her way through crowded halls full of high school students, wearing a Modesto Police Explorer uniform with a badge pinned to her chest. To stave off boredom, Chandra had signed up to volunteer with the police department and was relishing every minute of it, as she was drawn toward order and justice. Typically, young interns spent time handing out fines for littering, but Chandra insisted on shadowing cops as they did their rounds.

On weekends, she offered to go undercover and nab grocery stores selling alcohol to minors. So what if it wasn't cool? If Chandra had watched *Beverly Hills, 90210*, a TV show that was wildly popular with American teens in the nineties, she wouldn't have related to Kelly or Brenda, the female characters who talked about nothing but shopping and boys. Instead, she would have been drawn to Andrea Zuckerman, the Jewish journalism intern, who was nerdy, socially conscious, perpetually single.

Like Zuckerman, Chandra wanted to be a journalist, and she landed an internship with the sports section of her local newspaper, *The Modesto Bee*. She also developed a keen interest in astronomy and began taking college courses to earn university credits in her last years of high school. She wasn't into any of the boys at school, had no interest in standing out and waving pom-poms with the cheerleaders, and didn't give a hoot about prom. In her senior yearbook, in 1995, she wrote, "Always have dreams, always make them reality."

In a few years, Chandra was going to be the person her peers admired from afar, on social media, once she was an FBI agent, lawyer, or congressperson. They wouldn't be surprised, just a little jealous. She planned to show up to her ten-year high school reunion with her head held high.

Halfway through the flight, past Iowa, she could see the landscape shift from arid expanses to lush fields and wooded hills. Soon the plane would fly over the Great Lakes and then the forests of West Virginia. This wasn't Chandra's first time leaving the nest. After high school, she'd already gotten a first, albeit more modest, start, when she attended San Francisco State University, only one hundred miles from home.

She'd lived there for three years, in a small apartment off campus, as she had little interest in the promiscuity of dorm life, where students walked around in bathrobes, down musty halls, and where you had to share your room with a stranger.

Unlike other Californian universities and colleges, San Francisco State was not a party school. It was better known for welcoming adult students, people who were already working. The school was a good fit for Chandra, and she got her degree after three studious years. During this time, she also worked as the sports editor for her college newspaper and found she didn't enjoy her forays into professional journalism. To Chandra, journalists were too cynical. As her graduation date drew closer, she changed her mind, opting to pursue public administration instead.

During her undergrad years, Chandra also experienced her first heartbreak—not over a student, but with a cop who was ten years older than her. The relationship surprised no one, as Chandra had been into older men since high school. Her friend Channaly had even mentioned it in their senior yearbook: "Older guys are better! I mean, so what if Harrison F. is in his fifties? [. . .] Viva Brad! Viva older men!"

Chandra was determined, ambitious, and stable, and she'd always been drawn to men who shared these same traits. The boys in high school and college didn't meet her standards, but Mark Steele did. He was almost thirty years old, bright and handsome, with a promising future in the police force. Their relationship lasted two years, and Chandra even introduced him to her parents.

Meanwhile, at the police station, no one heard a peep about their relationship for the entire time they were together. It's quite remarkable, given that everyone who worked there acknowledged the place was an absolute rumor mill.

Chandra was discreet; her relationships were her business. At school, she didn't talk about Mark much either, although she'd often go back to Modesto on weekends to see him. He was her first love, and she thought she'd found "the one." At the end of the day, though, Chandra was still a naive twenty-year-old, and this tended to be most obvious when she was lovestruck. Sure, she was

PROLOGUE

sensible and mature for her age, but she had a blind spot when it came to the men she fell for.

When Chandra set her mind to something, it was hard to convince her to change course. Like when she became a vegetarian at fourteen—she'd stuck with it, even though she was the only one in the family. When she wanted something, she worked for it, stubbornly sank her teeth in, and never gave up. And she tended to come out stronger for it.

In the summer of her thirteenth birthday, for instance, her mother had forced her to take a climbing course with other kids her age. They were mostly boys, who snickered whenever she was around. By the end of the program, she was one of the only participants who hadn't dropped out.

So when Mark told her it was over, in August 1999, her first instinct was to cling to the relationship. But love doesn't work that way. You have to learn to let go, to give up, and to recognize when you've made a mistake. It was hard for Chandra, but she got there. Within a year, Mark Steele had married someone else. To comfort Chandra, Susan took her on a train ride through the Rocky Mountains. She used the opportunity to teach her daughter that when one door closes, another one opens. To move forward, sometimes you have to look in another direction. And so Chandra moved on.

Soon she had something new to focus on. While getting her master's degree in public administration at the University of Southern California (USC), she interned with Richard Riordan, the Republican mayor of Los Angeles. The following year, she landed another internship in Sacramento, in the office of Democratic governor Gray Davis.

For her next and final internship, Chandra didn't think twice: It was going to be Washington, DC, or bust. She sent her application to the US Bureau of Prisons, but also called up recruiter Daniel Dunne, to whom she explained that she didn't want "just any internship" and was seeking a truly rewarding experience that would "advance her career." Dunne was sold and immediately offered her a highly coveted internship with a $27,000 annual salary, way above average.

Chandra was certain that in the nation's epicenter, the bustling heart of American politics, she wouldn't have to be her parents' daughter anymore, the dedicated student, the small-town Californian. In Washington, DC, she could be whoever she wanted to be. Start fresh. Out there, with the exception of Jennifer Baker, a friend from college, she knew nobody. And this meant that no one would know her. The United Airlines Boeing 777 was taking her far away from herself, and she was ready.

PROLOGUE

As the plane began its descent, the landscape came into focus. From the vicinity of the airport, she couldn't see the Capitol, the White House, or even the Pentagon, but it didn't matter. All Chandra had to do was close her eyes to see them. She thought back to something her mother had said while helping to pack her suitcase. Susan wasn't the nosy type and tended to give Chandra her privacy. She even admired her daughter's independence. Still, it was hard to watch her move so far away. As she folded one of Chandra's little black tops, a sleeveless garment with a high collar, Susan blurted, "Don't you become another Monica Lewinsky!"

For the past two years, President Clinton's young mistress had been all over TV and on the front pages of the tabloids. She was the butt of talk show jokes and the topic of drunken conversations. Just eight months before, Congress had even voted to impeach the president for perjury and obstruction of justice. Chandra Levy and Monica Lewinsky did look quite similar. They were both brunettes, pretty, from well-to-do families, and the daughters of doctors. They were both Jewish, intelligent, and ambitious, attracted to men, *real* men, and drawn to the bright lights of Washington, DC. In response, Chandra just rolled her eyes. *Come on, Mom . . .*

Now at the other end of the country, she was already done thinking about it. Through the window, Chandra could finally see the Potomac River, which bordered the nation's capital. She heard the wheels hit the tarmac. She'd made it. In a few days, Chandra would begin her internship at the Federal Bureau of Prisons, on Capitol Hill, at the heart of the United States government. Her mecca. The date was September 14, 2000. Chandra's first day in Washington, DC.

THE WOMAN WHO VANISHED FROM DUPONT CIRCLE

1.
SEVEN MONTHS IN DC

TWO HUNDRED TWENTY-EIGHT DAYS LATER: CHANDRA'S LAST DAY IN WASHINGTON, DC

On May 1, 2001, Chandra Levy awoke in her apartment. Through the third-floor window, she looked out at a clear sky. She logged onto her bright blue Sony laptop and surfed the web from 10:27 a.m. to 12:24 p.m. Then she vanished into thin air. No one would ever see her again.

It was October in the Dupont Circle neighborhood. The leaves had begun to turn, and spooky Halloween decorations were strung up. A young woman pushed open the door of the Newport, a nice building at 1260 21st Street NW. She was dressed in athletic wear, with a bottle in hand and headphones on. It was easy to picture Chandra in this scene, looking content, active, splitting her Sunday between a workout at her favorite gym, the Washington Sports Club on Connecticut Avenue, and a stroll through the organic farmers' market that popped up every Sunday morning by the Metro.

When Chandra was in Washington, the Newport was full of young, active people, about two hundred of them, spread over nine floors. Most were in Washington for their first job on Capitol Hill. The White House, Congress, the Supreme Court, and the Bureau of Prisons were all just a few Metro stops away.

Chandra's apartment, door number 315, was a 484-square-foot studio that cost $1,400 a month. It had big windows and an open kitchen, an office nook, and a bed tucked into an alcove. She kept a small TV stored in a white cabinet.

Chandra had established a routine in DC, each day much like the one before it. After a morning session at the gym, she would leave the Newport, with her badge around her neck and her curly hair bouncing around her face. She would walk to the Metro, happy to have made a space for herself in this bustling city. She would arrive at the Bureau of Prisons, at 320 First Street NW, a large Art Deco–inspired corner building, and make her way up to the sixth floor to the Public Information Office. Then, she would settle in, read all news articles related to the ninety-eight federal prisons in the country and write up a summary for her boss, answer the phone, respond to emails, process media requests, and handle petitions from death row inmates. Every day was the same. And every day, Chandra was happy with the routine and her DC life.

She befriended twenty-eight-year-old colleague Sven Jones, and together they joked in the hallways and talked sports. At the Washington Sports Club, she also met Robert Kurkjian, twenty-eight years old, a former USC student, like her. He often suggested they go out, but most of the time she turned him down. Chandra had always surrounded herself with male friends rather than girlfriends. As far back as high school, she'd found teenage girls superficial and cruel. In Washington, it was even worse. She told her mother how the women in this new city were cutthroat and highly competitive, how they looked each other up and down, and how they vied for the few spots left behind by the men. Chandra preferred not to get involved in their games.

Fortunately, she had Jennifer Baker, a friend from USC who was also from Modesto, and they spent their weekends together. Jennifer was a petite brunette with a sleek bob parted down the middle. Together, they walked for hours through Washington, enjoying the dozens of vegetarian restaurants in the capital, checking out museums, and talking about their plans for the future.

Both young women were ambitious. They wanted to land permanent jobs in Washington, to settle down there, and build solid careers for themselves. To develop their networks, they organized what they called "political field trips," where they would, for example, get tickets to attend a debate organized by CNN at Georgetown University. Other days, they'd show up unannounced at the local offices of members of Congress to chat with their staff and start making contacts.

One day in October, they dropped by the office of Congressman Gary Condit, who was the Democratic representative for Modesto, California, and one of the most prominent politicians in Washington. It was the start of a new school year in 2000, and Condit, aged fifty-two, was getting ready to be elected for a seventh term in the House of Representatives. He was delighted to meet two of his constituents and gave them a tour of his office, then brought them to the House gallery to watch a vote. They got a photo together, and Jennifer, who had been out of work that morning, landed an internship at Condit's Washington office. Not a bad day.

Meanwhile, Chandra pulled every string she had. By leveraging her California roots, she managed to book a meeting with Democratic senator Barbara Boxer. In a photo taken on the day they met, she is wearing the necklace her parents gave her in Israel—she never went anywhere without it—and the same little fine-knit blue top she had worn to Condit's office. Looking somewhat shy, but proud of herself, she has a little smile that brings out her cheekbones.

On Election Day, November 7, 2000, Chandra and Jennifer left work and hurried over to Hawk 'n' Dove, a local institution where young Capitol Hill workers met for beers. It was a tight race between George W. Bush and Al Gore. By 8:00 p.m., exit polls suggested Gore would take Florida, with the entire election hinging on this state. By 10:00 p.m., projections had made a full one-eighty. At 2:30 a.m., several news channels claimed Bush had won, but they retracted their statements at 4:30 a.m. In the end, it would take over a month to settle the matter.

As Chandra and Jennifer made their way home from the bar, winding down after a feverish night, they looked out over the lights of the Capitol. Then, they returned to Dupont Circle feeling elated.

On May 11, 2001, Chandra was planning to go back to California for her graduation, where she would stay for a few days. The idea was to meet up with her parents, grandmother, and brother in Modesto, then fly to Los Angeles together. For the first part of the trip, she planned to take a train across the country, starting in Washington, DC. It would be long—two or three days—but she'd heard it was worth it. She'd always dreamed of seeing the country this way.

By the time May 6 came around, Chandra's parents had not heard from their daughter in a week. They were annoyed. Sure, Chandra was independent, but she could have let them know what she was up to. Should they wait for her in Modesto, as planned? When would she arrive? Was she taking a plane or a train in the end? Her father, Bob, left one message after another on her answering machine. On Sunday, he began to feel dread in the pit of his stomach. It was unlike her to go silent.

So Bob called the front desk clerk at the Newport, as he would have seen all the tenants' daily comings and goings. But the employee refused to enter apartment 315. It wasn't his business. Chandra was an adult, wasn't she? Bob hung up. He had no other choice—his next call would be to the DC police. Panic set in as he told them about his daughter, who had given them no sign of life.

THE WOMAN WHO VANISHED FROM DUPONT CIRCLE

A few hours later, the police sent a patrol to the Newport apartments, and the building manager let them into unit 315. The studio was empty. Two suitcases lay on the floor, open and half filled with clothes. Other outfits were still hanging in the closet. A comforter had been left on the floor in the entryway. In the fridge, they found leftover pasta and Reese's peanut butter cups. Stranger still, they noticed her phone and wallet were in the apartment, with her credit card, driver's license, and some cash. They found the necklace her parents had given her, the one she wore everywhere, and her laptop was open on the desk. End of police report. Now Bob was having trouble breathing.

The cops were slow to call back. The FBI wasn't answering. The Newport security guard figured his job was done. Chandra Levy was officially a missing person, but no one seemed to give a damn. After all, tons of adults vanished in DC. Most of them came back. Others were less fortunate. America's capital had a high crime rate, so a missing person was always less urgent than the previous night's murders. And, in Washington, not a single night went by without at least one murder.

Still, posters were printed and put up around the neighborhood. They showed Chandra's face and her full name: Chandra Ann Levy. On May 10, a press release was issued. Journalists made a note of it, then moved on. If the kid didn't turn up, it could be a good story for a quiet day.

Then a rumor began to float around. No one quite knew where it had come from or how it had taken off, but it was there, on the breeze. It spread from one newsroom to the next, maybe over the phone, maybe in whispered conversations. Within just a few days, the rumor had settled in, as if it'd always been there. In Washington, people were saying that the missing Dupont Circle girl had been sleeping with a congressman.

But, then again, it was 2001, in the US capital . . . This type of story was old news. In fact, sex between young women and politicians was practically a local sport, and tales of infidelity went back all the way to the days of the founding fathers. In the more recent past, US presidents Franklin D. Roosevelt, Lyndon B. Johnson, and John F. Kennedy had all had affairs. One of Kennedy's mistresses had been a nineteen-year-old intern.

Every summer, a wave of ambitious and impressionable young women rolled into Washington. In their eyes, the elected officials on Capitol Hill were like rock stars. Rock stars with families that lived far away, in their respective constituencies. Rock stars who were lonely . . . Even more practical was the fact that these girls tended to leave town after a few months, only to be replaced by a new generation of fresh faces. In the 1960s, this had earned them the nickname "ninety-day wonders." Now, at the start of a new millennium, people called the young women "staff ass."

Interns and politicians often mingled in the halls of Capitol Hill, at the endless buffets organized by lobbyists and in local bars and restaurants. It was so easy to have an affair and even easier to think that all parties were getting something out of it.

When Chandra Levy disappeared in May 2001, the world's most high-profile affair was, of course, Bill Clinton's relationship with White House intern Monica Lewinsky. When their liaison had begun in 1995, Lewinsky was twenty-two years old. The president was forty-nine. Three years later, in 1998, it was the scandal of the year. The whole world seemed to revolve around this one story. And people treated it like a joke. In the fall after the affair came out, Halloween stores were flooded with requests for "Monica costumes." After every detail of their story had been dissected, thong purchases exploded, making them the best-selling product in the American lingerie industry.

President Clinton's popularity tracked in the same direction, and in February 1998, at the height of the scandal, his ratings rose to 71 percent. Viagra, the little blue pill, had just come on the market, male sexuality was having a moment, and the president's actions were deemed a sign of virility. In 2001, when Chandra Levy disappeared, the scandal was still fresh in everyone's minds.

She was the keeper of Chandra's secrets. Linda Zamsky is Chandra's aunt and the wife of Susan Levy's brother. Her home in Chesapeake City, Maryland, backs onto a lush yard with a lake that borders the neighboring homes. Outside, her dogs are playing rough and she calls out to them, quickly bringing them back into line.

Zamsky is a whirlwind. Tall, energetic, and outspoken, she seems like the kind of person you wouldn't want to cross. The phone rings, and she moves briskly to answer the call. It's the medical office she manages in town—they need her to find a replacement nurse. She calls the dogs in, sits back down, then gets up and offers drinks. Only when she agrees to sit down do her eyes finally settle, her tall figure coming to rest.

In a husky voice, she whispers, "We sat at this table here, she was sitting where you're sitting." The round table in the kitchen is by a window with a view of the lake. Nothing has changed in this room since that Thanksgiving weekend in 2000. Linda tries to count the years in her head, without really wanting to know the answer to her question. It was in fact twenty-three years ago.

Chandra had been looking out over this landscape when she told Linda she'd met someone. Her niece had come over for the holidays. She liked to walk through the wide, open spaces in Maryland, and she got along well with Zamsky, who, at forty, was about ten years younger than her parents. They often called each other to chat, especially since Chandra had moved out east.

"She said this guy was older, and married," Zamsky recalls. She wasn't one to judge. At the time, she'd just shrugged, at most. Her own husband was fourteen years older than her, and the age gap had been even bigger with her ex-husband. With Zamsky, Chandra felt free to express her preference for mature men. But she wouldn't say his name. He was an important person. When Zamsky asked how old he was, Chandra told her he was "fiftyish." She didn't seem to have any qualms about the fact that he was married.

Chandra figured his wife didn't make him happy, that the poor man needed something more. Soon, she would tell her aunt that their marriage was only a facade, a young love that had long since turned into a partnership and strategic companionship. Chandra's logic was typical of a young person: If people loved each other, they wouldn't cheat. So, if he was unfaithful, it had to mean they weren't in love anymore. It was a classic Sophist argument.

At this Thanksgiving dinner in 2000, Chandra was radiant. The next day, she and her aunt went shopping, and Chandra talked about "her man" again. "How do you get in touch with him if it's so secretive?" asked Zamsky. Chandra explained that she had to dial up a special number that never rang and, instead, played a kind of elevator music until it went to voicemail. She'd leave a message, then wait for him to call her back.

But sometimes she also called his office. "Then they'd answer 'Congressman Gary Condit's office' and I . . . Oops." Chandra turned to her aunt. "You didn't hear that, did you?" Zamsky was a vault. In any case, the name Gary Condit didn't ring a bell. She didn't really follow politics.

Today, two decades later, her gaze is lost in the distance. She points to a tree standing a little taller than the rest. "I call it the Chandra tree. When I pass by, I say, 'Hi Chandra.' A friend gave me the tree when she went . . ." She trails off. Then, she adds, as if to herself, "Everyone needs someone to keep their secrets."

The relationship began about six weeks before Thanksgiving. When Chandra walked into Condit's Washington office with Jennifer Baker, she thought the fifty-two-year-old congressman looked like Harrison Ford. Something about his hair, maybe. Then she ran into him a second time a few days later while popping in to see Jennifer, who was interning for the congressman. On that day, Chandra, a student, and Condit, a married man, exchanged numbers and email addresses.

Chandra wasted no time and soon called him to ask for career advice. By the end of the conversation, they'd agreed to meet for dinner. They met at Tryst, a coffee shop on 18th Street NW that was popular with government workers. It was in the trendy Adams Morgan neighborhood, just minutes from Condit's place, a condo unit on the fourth floor of an elegant white-columned building. Soon, Chandra would be spending two to three nights a week in that apartment.

The relationship had to be kept a secret, so there were rules to follow. Tell no one, of course. Not her friends, especially Jennifer, not her family, and not her colleagues either. When Chandra came to his place, if she crossed paths with a neighbor in the elevator, she was to stay on for one more floor, then say she was coming to visit a sick friend. When they went out—rarely—she was expected to wear a baseball cap and rush into the taxi at the last second so they wouldn't be seen together. Then, inside the taxi, they would not say a word.

If they were meeting somewhere, Chandra had to go without ID and take as few things as possible. To reach Condit, she always had to dial the secret number with the elevator music, then patiently wait for him to call back. If he didn't call back, it meant he wasn't free. *He* decided when they could see each other. And when they did, they spent most of their time together in the Adams Morgan apartment, getting pasta delivered from Pasta Mia (Condit's favorite restaurant), eating chocolate chip cookie dough ice cream (Condit's favorite), watching HBO, and discussing the latest political news, even though, in reality, Chandra was more interested in this than Condit.

Chandra's life essentially boiled down to three things: working, going to the gym, and spending time at Condit's place. She didn't get out much, because she wanted to be free when he called. She saw less and less of Jennifer and told her she was dating an FBI agent. Chandra

THE WOMAN WHO VANISHED FROM DUPONT CIRCLE

diligently abided by all the rules. She was patient, obedient, devoted, and asked for nothing more.

Condit appreciated these qualities and told her it was nice to have someone who "[understood] his way of life" and that he hadn't always been so lucky in his previous relationships. *Previous relationships?* Chandra realized she was not his first mistress. Perhaps she took it as a sign that his marriage had been over for a long time. More importantly, he seemed to be saying she was better than the others. So, when Condit told her she could see other men if she wanted to, Chandra turned down the offer; she wanted the relationship to be exclusive.

❖

President George W. Bush's inauguration was held on January 20, 2001. It was a cold and rainy morning. The new president and his predecessor, Bill Clinton, were dressed the same, in matching long black coats, blue ties, white shirts—as if to show that, in America, nothing ever truly changes.

That day, Robert Kurkjian got a call from Chandra. He was surprised. They weren't particularly close and rarely saw one another outside of the gym where they both worked out. "I have tickets to the Inaugural Ball tonight. Are you free?" Kurkjian, who always kept a tuxedo in his closet just in case, accepted the invitation.

When he came to pick her up, Chandra told him they first had to stop by her "boyfriend's" place to pick up their tickets. He wondered why her boyfriend wasn't accompanying her and why Chandra had told him, with a touch of authority, to stay in the car. But he kept these thoughts to himself. He parked in front of the Adams Morgan building and waited until Chandra came down with an envelope in hand.

The ball was held in the lobby of the National Museum of Women in the Arts, a stunning room made of light marble and flanked by two sweeping staircases. Glittering chandeliers hung from the ceiling, and the walls were lined with art pieces in gilded frames. Kurkjian and Chandra made their way upstairs and watched the party below. Chandra wasn't particularly interested in the bar and the flutes of champagne, nor in the dance floor, where the lucky guests were grooving, happy to be a part of this momentous occasion.

As Chandra scanned the crowd, Kurkjian realized she was looking for something. He started to wonder what he was even doing there and eventually asked about her mysterious boyfriend, this man who was powerful enough to get her two tickets to one of DC's most exclusive parties but was unwilling to be her date. "He's a member of Congress," Chandra let slip. That was the only bit of information that would come out of the conversation. Kurkjian wanted to know whether he was a Democrat or a Republican, which state he represented, how long he had been in Congress, and whether he was married, but Chandra systematically said she couldn't say.

Eventually, he, too, began to scan the crowd. The congressman had to be there. Did Kurkjian understand that he was just some date, someone Chandra could have on her arm while she came here to spy on "her guy"? And did Chandra feel like she was sharing a part of the experience with Condit, the person she actually wanted to walk through the door with? When Kurkjian told the story to *Washington Post* journalists years later, he recalled feeling that night that Chandra's life revolved entirely around this man. And that mostly he found it sad.

Today, Sven Jones is fifty. Chandra's former colleague no longer speaks to the press and is protective of his online presence. He doesn't work for the government anymore either and switched to another field, where he's an independent contractor. In a single text message, he explains that for a decade, he was "unemployable" because his name was associated with the "Chandra case," and this put him in an awkward position. He'll never forget Chandra, but he can't get pulled back into the case again.

Many memories must haunt Jones, perhaps one more than the rest. It was a morning in early April. Chandra was upset when she arrived at the office. She told Jones she had "a problem," but when he offered to help, she tensed up. "No, it's a female problem," she countered. Sven had boundaries, and he let it go. He got the impression she would settle this with a doctor, though she hadn't said as much. She assured him it was nothing she couldn't handle on her own. So, Jones changed the topic and they moved on. He never did find out what she meant by "female problem."

At the office, Jones also heard a lot about this mystery congressman. Chandra wondered what she should get him for his birthday. What do you give a fifty-year-old married man who is not your father? She also repeatedly told Jones that her lover's marriage was just a formality. His wife lived thousands of miles away, and their marriage was unfulfilling. Jones understood that, on some level, Chandra liked this illicit side of the relationship. It spiced things up. And the "sex was pretty intense," she once confided.

But over time, he noticed Chandra becoming depressed. She wondered: What if all this never led to a real relationship? What if she could never experience this happiness publicly? In April 2001, when Chandra went back to her aunt's house for Passover, she wore a gold bracelet, "a very nice piece of jewelry," Zamsky recalls. Condit had given it to her for Valentine's Day. It seemed the relationship had taken a more serious turn since Chandra and Zamsky had last seen each other. Chandra was now talking about a five-year plan.

Imitating her niece, Zamsky gestures as she speaks, using her hands to put imaginary things in order. The plan was simple: In May, Chandra would go home to California to pick up her diploma, then she'd come back, finish her internship, and find a job in DC. For five years, the couple would continue to date in secret. This would give Chandra time to pour all her energy and free time into her work, and land her dream job.

Next, her congressman would leave politics and his wife to start a career in lobbying. And finally, they would be able to build a new family together. In five years, Chandra would be almost twenty-nine years old. She had always wanted children, and felt this left her plenty of time. Some days, she felt the timeline even seemed a little long, but Zamsky reassured her—Chandra was still young, everything would be fine.

This wasn't the first time Chandra was trying to make the relationship as official as possible despite the circumstances. In January, she had written to her Newport landlord, asking how she could end her lease, as she was planning to move in with her partner. When the owner called her back to discuss the matter on February 1, Chandra backtracked. "It didn't work out," she told him.

Sven Jones, on the other hand, had more reservations about this five-year plan and tried to warn Chandra. Sometimes husbands leave their wives, but . . . not often. "And even if he does, do you want to be with a powerful man who is thirty years older than you? And if he's cheating on his wife, who's to say he won't cheat on you?"

The more they talked about it, the more Jones realized that Chandra wanted something else too. She needed a faster, deeper commitment. In the final weeks before her disappearance, the two colleagues talked about one thing only: how to get the congressman to leave his wife. They cooked up plans, with the right wording, the right timing. One day, Jones would see her come in angry, ready to punch a table. The next, she would be soothed, placated by a few nice words. Within a few days, the cycle would start over again. This time, Chandra would be sure—she was "determined to have this confrontation," and intended to present her demands to Condit.

As her friend, Jones warned her not to press him. "If you push a man like that too hard, he's going to feel as if he's lost some control. If you really want to hook this guy, you should lie low and let him feel like he's making the decisions."

But Chandra couldn't play it cool anymore. Her reply was sharp. "I've invested too much in this [relationship]."

April was also Chandra's birthday month. On the fourteenth, she turned twenty-four. Her parents came to meet her at her aunt's house for Passover, and they spent her birthday at her godmother's home in Pennsylvania. Today, Chandra's mother Susan remembers a pleasant day spent together at the spa. They'd shared a chocolate cake decorated with flowers, then thunderstorms had broken out.

During this vacation, Chandra had used her aunt's and her father's phones to make calls to DC. She'd joked about her secret lover. The whole family seemed to understand he was a man of power, but no one pressed her for more details. They knew Chandra would spill nothing.

In one of the photos taken that day, Susan and Chandra are sitting close together on a black leather couch. It's hard to tell which brown curls belong to whom. Susan rests her head on her daughter's shoulder, and both have their eyes closed. It looks like an imperfect photo of a perfect moment.

❖

When Chandra got back to Washington, the office was buzzing. Timothy McVeigh's execution had been scheduled for June. A Gulf War veteran, McVeigh was sentenced to death for the 1995 bombing of a federal building in Oklahoma City. The attack killed 168 people. In the spring of 2001, it was still the deadliest act of terrorism in the history of the United States.

At the Bureau of Prisons, the phone was ringing nonstop, and Chandra was helping organize a press conference. But on Monday, April 23, her carefully planned career trajectory hit an unexpected road bump. In a conversation by the coffee machine, Chandra mentioned to one of her managers that she had completed all her university credits in December and that she would soon go home to California to attend her official graduation ceremony with her classmates. Suddenly, the personnel officer balked—the Bureau of Prisons, like many government offices, only allowed internships within four months of graduation. If Chandra had technically graduated in December, then her internship could not go beyond April. There was no way she'd be allowed to stay on until September, as she'd planned. Her contract was terminated on the spot, and within a few short minutes, Chandra was out of a job.

The next morning, on Tuesday, April 24, she went to Condit's place and told him what had happened. She explained how she'd probably have to move back to California. She had recently applied to work as an FBI analyst but likely wouldn't hear back for a while. She told him maybe she could start law school or find a job in Sacramento, where she had contacts. According to Condit, who reluctantly described this encounter to journalists, they met for roughly an hour and a half. He claimed Chandra was disappointed but didn't seem desperate. He couldn't remember if they'd had sex that day.

On Friday, April 27, she called her parents in California. She'd used this unexpected free time to see the Holocaust Museum and wanted to tell them about her experience. During the conversation, she told her mother about losing the internship, saying, "It's not what I would have wanted, but that's the way it is."

That evening, she asked Robert Kurkjian to get a drink with her at a bar. It was her last weekend in DC, and she begged him to come out. But Kurkjian was tired and already had plans to order a pizza and watch a movie with his roommate. When he suggested she come by for a drink, he was sure she'd turn him down, as she'd already turned him down twice since the Inaugural Ball. But Chandra took him up on the offer. Clearly, she didn't feel like spending the evening alone. And she wanted to talk.

As soon as she arrived, Chandra poured her heart out, disappointed to be leaving Washington—and her lover. She laid out the five-year plan. Her guy would get a divorce, he'd leave politics, they'd start a second family . . . Kurkjian resisted the urge to roll his eyes. He couldn't believe Chandra, who seemed to have a good head on her shoulders, could be so hopelessly naive. Gently, he tried to tell her that this mystery congressman didn't care about her. But Chandra wasn't having it. So, they watched *The 6th Day* and then, at about 1:00 a.m., Kurkjian walked her to the end of the street, where she hailed a cab to take her the few blocks home. That was the last time he saw her.

On Saturday, April 28, she called Sven Jones to suggest getting lunch together the following Monday. Jones didn't pick up, so she left a message on his answering machine. When he later listened to the message—he was in Canada that weekend—Jones thought she sounded sad and wondered if she was still depressed over her lover.

But since he wouldn't be back by Monday, he didn't return the call.

At 11:14 p.m., Chandra sent an email to her landlord. "It looks like my plans have suddenly changed. I was just informed this week that my job appointment time is up so I am out of work. I'm moving back [to California] for good. I would like to vacate the apartment on May 5 or 6 if possible. I really hate giving up the apartment, but I think I need to be in California for a while to figure out what my next move is."

On Sunday, April 29, Chandra made at least two phone calls. Gary Condit would eventually admit that they talked to each other that day. About what? About nothing, according to him. It was just a normal, boring conversation. He asked her when she was going back to California, and she told him "next week" but that she hadn't bought a ticket yet. The call was brief. And for good reason—Condit's wife was in DC that day. She had arrived the evening before and was planning to stay until Thursday, May 3.

Chandra's second call was to her aunt Linda, and she left her a message. "Hi, Linda. This is Chandra. My internship is over. I'm planning on packing my bags in the next week or ten days. Heading home for a while, don't know what I'm going to do this summer. And I really have some big news or something important to tell. Call me." Linda Zamsky has listened to this message many times. On the tape, Chandra sounds like a happy and excited young woman.

On Monday, April 30, Chandra went to her regular gym to cancel her membership. She spent a while talking to the manager in the lobby. She told him she was heading back to California and asked if there were any affiliate gyms out there, since her membership would last through the month. That Monday, she called her own voicemail several times—at least seven or eight attempts—to see if she had any messages. Linda hadn't called back.

On Tuesday, May 1, Chandra got on her computer and connected to the internet. The time was 10:27 a.m. She went to the Amtrak and Southwest Airlines websites. At 10:45 a.m., she forwarded an email to her parents. It was an advertisement for discounted flights between Modesto and Los Angeles. She sent the email without adding any comment.

She checked out a few news sites, like *The Los Angeles Times*, *The Hollywood Reporter*, *Drudge Report*, *The Modesto Bee*, and *National Geographic*, and read articles about a White House luncheon that Condit had attended on an invitation by President Bush. She also read a couple articles about Gary's children, Chad and

Cadee Condit, aged thirty-three and twenty-six. She looked up a map of Baskin-Robbins locations. Multiple search engines were used: Google, Lycos, Yahoo, AltaVista. The pace was frantic, and she sometimes stayed on a page for just a few seconds.

Finally, at 11:26 a.m., Chandra checked the weather forecast on the *Washington Post* website. It was May 1, and the sky was clear, with an expected high of 81°F. Next, she clicked on the "Entertainment Guide" menu and browsed some pages about Rock Creek Park and its hiking trails. Strangely, she also looked up information about the Alsace-Lorraine region, in France. At 12:24 p.m., she logged off.

This would be the last sign of life from Chandra Levy.

2.
CHANDRA DRAMA

SUMMER 2001

When Americans look back on it, they think of three things. It was the last summer before everything fell apart: a time of innocence, of an America that was still proud and arrogant. It was the summer of sharks. In and around Florida, five lethal attacks had made headlines, including an iconic front cover of *Time* magazine that was reminiscent of *Jaws*. (The truth was, there had been more than twice as many attacks over the previous summer, but newspapers at the time had been busy covering elections, not sharks.) And the summer of 2001 was the summer of Chandra Levy.

Chandra's disappearance had become the "Chandra Levy case." The twenty-four-hour news networks—CNN, as well as Fox News and MSNBC, which had been launched only five years earlier—ran with the story.

A decade before, the Gulf War had made its way into television coverage. As the country's first dedicated news channel, CNN had offered live updates, turning more than half of Americans into news junkies. But then the war had lasted only a few months. So, what was an insatiable audience to do? As Allison Yarrow writes in *90s Bitch: Media, Culture, and the Failed Promise of Gender Equality*, "All [the news channels] needed was another war. But soon they would learn that political dramas, crime, and Hollywood were far cheaper to cover, and often more popular, than bombs over Baghdad."

They were in luck. The years preceding Chandra's disappearance were rife with scandals that could be turned into binge-worthy TV shows. Dozens of people died in the Los Angeles riots, which had been triggered by the acquittal of the police officers who beat Rodney King; Lorena Bobbitt was thrust into the national spotlight after cutting off her husband's penis when he attempted to rape her; a friend and member of the Clinton administration, Vince Foster, was found dead in a park; the first pedophilia charges were filed against Michael Jackson;

Prince Charles and Princess Diana announced their divorce; rapper Tupac Shakur was murdered.

In 1994, O. J. Simpson was arrested for the murder of his ex-wife, a story that ninety-five million Americans watched unfold, live. The birth of the twenty-four-hour news cycle, and the use of live reporting, have since been attributed to his trial, which lasted 134 days and was entirely live-broadcasted. Many people have analyzed the way in which the media covered the O. J. Simpson case and published their theories about it. At the end of the day, all parties agree on one thing: The case marked the beginning of a golden age for tabloids, an era of media overkill that lives on to this day.

But what sold even better than crime was sex. Monica Lewinsky and Anita Hill—the woman who testified at Clarence Thomas's 1991 Supreme Court nomination hearing to accuse him of sexual harassment—both experienced this reality. *They* were the ones shown on every TV station, just like Pamela Anderson and the world's first sex tape, Anna Nicole Smith, who brought Playmates to fame, Lolo Ferrari and her record-breaking breasts . . . It was the women, and not the men involved in the stories, who were judged, scrutinized, criticized, and mocked.

In the nineties, and early aughts, women covered by the media were bound to lose. They were inevitably deemed too sexy like Monica Lewinsky and Pamela Anderson, too cold like Anita Hill and Hillary Clinton, too crazy like Britney Spears, too angry like Tonya Harding, too skinny like Calista Flockhart from *Ally McBeal*, too fat like, *again*, Monica Lewinsky, and too competent like Marcia Clark, the prosecutor in the O. J. Simpson trial who was judged so mercilessly that she walked away from her career.

Women and sex are intrinsically linked, and America is and was obsessed with both. Allison Yarrow sums it up this way: "It was in this climate of abysmal sex education, coercion, violence, shame, and blame that sex scandals replaced baseball as the national pastime."

And so, the Chandra Levy case came to be known as "the Chandra Drama." Five times an hour, CNN, MSNBC, and Fox would report on the story. It didn't take long for journalists to figure out that the alleged affair was tied to Condit. Chandra was from his district, there was a photo of them with Jennifer Baker, and the congressman had been questioned by the police.

At the time, Michael Doyle was a forty-something reporter specializing in California politics. He was the Washington correspondent for the Sacramento-based McClatchy Media Company, which had many news outlets, including *The Modesto Bee*. He vividly recalls the stiff competition between journalists. Everyone wanted the scoop, "but there was a hierarchy of reporters," he says.

At the top of the pyramid were *Washington Post* reporters Sari Horwitz, Scott Higham, and Allan Lengel. "Jerks . . ." says Doyle, with a chuckle. The journalist remembers resenting *The Washington Post*'s little crew for having all the contacts that other journalists could only dream of. They knew "the police, the local investigators, the prosecutor's office . . . they had everything. [. . .] They're incredible reporters. Sari is affirming, nice, body language—next thing you know, you're confessing your sins to her! Scott is dogged, exhaustive. I had a lot of respect for them, and I hated them with a passion."

Since he had no contacts in Washington, Doyle focused on what he knew best: California, state politics, and Gary Condit. Then he made a remarkable breakthrough. When Doyle contacted some of Chandra's former USC classmates, they shared emails from her that revealed vital information. He's kept them all in a big green folder. Twenty years later, he dusts it off and pulls out a loose sheet of paper on which he clumsily crossed out the recipient's last name.

On December 23, 2000, Chandra wrote this to her friend Jason: "My short trip to California wasn't much fun, I was sick when I was in Sacramento and I only got home for one night before I flew back to DC. The nice thing is that the man I'm seeing took care of my plane ticket for me!" Later, she goes on, "Everything else here in DC is going good [. . .] My man will be coming back here when Congress starts up again, I'm looking forward to seeing him."

The emails were presented in *The Fresno Bee* in an article published on May 18, 2001, and they went on to fuel rumors about Condit, who continued to deny having an affair with Chandra, insisting that they were merely "good friends." That afternoon, Doyle attended a press conference about the Chandra case. Everyone was congratulating him. He recalls, "I remember a TV producer saying, 'Good get, man, that was a good get.' [. . .] I had never heard that phrase before. And he said, 'Can I get [the emails]?'"

On May 16, when Bob and Susan Levy landed in Washington at 11:00 p.m., dozens of cameras were waiting for them. Photos from that day show Susan holding one of Chandra's favorite stuffed animals, a big yellow plush chick. From inside the taxi, Bob couldn't help but scan the streets of the capital, hoping to spot someone who looked like his daughter.

The trip had been organized by the Carole Sund/Carrington Memorial Reward Foundation, an organization founded to support the families of missing persons and which happened to be based in Modesto. On May 17, the organization held a first press conference at the Key Bridge Marriott in Arlington. Susan stood up straight and stoic, while Bob buried his face in her shoulder and sobbed.

George Arata, who had been both their friend and lawyer up to this point, had also arranged a meeting with a DC litigator named Billy Martin, a man whose picture was printed in glossy magazines and who had represented Monica Lewinsky's mother. From now on, he would be looking out for the Levy parents, and he quickly lay down new rules.

First, Martin hired a crack communications team made up of giants from Porter Novelli; then he called up Judy Smith, a crisis manager who was the inspiration for *Scandal*'s Olivia Pope. Going forward, the team would filter all media requests. Second, but no less important, from now on, the Levys were forbidden from talking to anyone about the case, even family and friends. And so began a full-blown marketing campaign. The goal: Sell Chandra to Americans.

Condit had also hired a prominent lawyer—Abbe Lowell, a Washington veteran who had been one of Bill Clinton's attorneys—and a team of communications experts. His career and family were at stake. The congressman's repeated denials were unconvincing, and nobody was buying his story about a "close friendship" between young Chandra and this powerful fifty-three-year-old married man, who had everything to lose if he admitted to an infidelity.

On June 6, *The Washington Post* reported that, according to a police source, Chandra sometimes spent the night at his condo in Adams Morgan. In response, Condit stubbornly stuck to his guns, reiterating that they were just friends. The people of DC rolled their eyes. In an attempt to shift media focus away from Condit, Marina Ein, his PR person, quietly suggested to reporters that *Talk* magazine was about to publish an article about how Chandra regularly had one-night stands. But the magazine denied this claim.

They were, in fact, working on an article, but it was absolutely not about *that*. The blunder cast a light on what the media immediately labeled a "Chandra smear campaign." Other attempts were more subtle. As early as May, Fox News reported on a tip from an "anonymous source," claiming Condit had gently "[broken] off his close friendship with Chandra" a few days before her disappearance, and that the young woman "refused to take no for an answer," was very "distraught," and became "obsessed with him." The source also told reporters that

Chandra had called the congressman several times, but he never returned her calls.

In reality, two messages from Condit were later found unopened on Chandra's answering machine, when the police finally searched her apartment. Despite this fact, the anonymous source's story was picked up by several other news outlets. Was the Condit camp trying to push the suicide theory, a theory that had briefly been considered by the police, that made Chandra out to be obsessive and depressed after losing her job and her boyfriend?

On the other side, the Chandra camp established two strategies. First, they would start by giving exclusive interviews to only the written press. The TV channels would follow—they always did. And, most importantly, they would not be sharing everything they knew about Chandra all at once. Instead, they wanted to gradually release details so the case would remain relevant for as long as possible.

"With a missing person case," recalls Judy Smith, as she sits in her car between appointments, "you want to make sure the public is aware. The media was a very crucial and important tool in that case. [. . .] One reason why [reporters] were interested was obviously the relationship involving Condit." In hindsight,

Smith feels the Condit camp made her job easier. "We recounted her story, showed who she was as a person, and I think the more the facts unraveled and people found out that Condit lied [. . .] that certainly helped make our point."

Bob and Susan Levy did what their lawyer asked of them. They spoke with journalists when they were told to and kept quiet when they were told to shut it down. They were distraught, didn't have the strength to go against Martin's orders, and they hoped that if they did everything right, maybe Chandra would be found alive. Maybe she'd finally come home to Modesto and walk through the front door, which they'd finally be able to close, shutting out the reporters squatting at the end of their driveway.

Linda Zamsky doesn't see it that way. She was frustrated that she'd been excluded, as were some of her niece's friends, like Sven Jones and Jennifer Baker, with whom Zamsky sometimes had phone conversations. Why wasn't anybody telling them anything about the investigation? Was it a communications strategy? The answer was simple: The Levy team did not trust Zamsky. She was too willful, too impulsive. To the smooth world of Washington, she was deemed not press-compatible.

In her home in Maryland, Zamsky paced like a lioness in a cage. She couldn't take Condit's lies anymore. He was hampering the investigation and obstructing the truth. And with its slow-release strategy, the Levy team was not providing irrefutable proof of the affair, giving Condit the opportunity to deny allegations. Chandra had been missing for two months . . . Wasn't it time the truth came out?

One morning in early July, Zamsky decided to shake things up in Washington. She accepted an interview request from *The Washington Post* and shared everything Chandra had told her in private. Yes, Chandra had named Gary Condit as her lover. Yes, it was an ongoing relationship. Yes, she had been staying the night at his place three times a week. Yes, they were sleeping together. Yes, they had a five-year plan in which the congressman was to leave his wife. Yes, he had given her gifts. Yes, he asked her to lie for him, always having her leave behind her ID. And yes, Gary Condit was a liar. Yes, yes, yes.

On July 6, the *Washington Post* article was published. With their hands tied, the Levy family's PR team issued a press release for all news outlets. Condit's California chief of staff, Mike Lynch, made his own statement, sending the ball back into Abbe Lowell's court. Lowell responded, returning the ball to Marina Ein. Now, Ein, who had recently attempted to mar Chandra's reputation, encouraged "the media to do everything possible to assist the police and focus on what [was] important, which [was] Chandra Levy." But if Ein thought the media circus had peaked by July 6, 2001, she would be astounded by what would follow.

By July 13, 63 percent of Americans were following the story closely, according to a CNN/*USA Today*/Gallup poll. Among those who followed the story "very closely," 47 percent deemed it "very likely" that Condit was directly involved in Chandra's disappearance. As for the tabloids, once all the details about the affair became known, the gloves came off and all hell broke loose.

In *Sex, Power & Murder*, a book featuring an astonishing compilation of articles by the *National Enquirer*—the number one tabloid at the time—statements like this one are made as early as page six: "'Chandra downloaded dozens of pictures showing breasts of different sizes,' revealed a DC police insider. 'The police didn't know what that meant, but investigators later found out that Condit is a breast man. Some investigators think that Chandra thought her breasts weren't nice enough for him and that maybe she was contemplating surgery to make him happy.'"

The *National Enquirer* also reached out to several psychiatrists, none of whom had met Chandra, to analyze her actions. Dr. Judianne Densen-Gerber stated, "She was no Virgin Mary. She manipulated men by her sexuality. Sex would mean very little to her except as a tool. Conquering older men made her feel powerful."

Meanwhile, psychologist Jamie Turndorf theorized that "when young women leave home, they don't leave behind things like their jewelry boxes [. . .] or cosmetics. But Chandra did—and it indicates that she had mixed feelings about growing up [. . .]. She had one foot in the adult world, but kept the other still planted firmly in her childhood. The mixed messages here are typical of a woman who could be lured into a liaison with a married man."

Another "expert," Dr. Carole Lieberman, added, "What women like her are acting out is missing a father figure. Fathers who are workaholics, like busy doctors, may love their daughters, but how much time can they give them throughout their childhood? By dating older men, she is looking for a true father figure to give her the full-time attention she never had. And why married men? That's to do with competition with her mother [. . .] She would be jealous that her mother was getting more [love and attention] than she was. [Condit was] a powerful daddy [. . .] to be won away from his wife [. . .] and she instantly saw him as a long-lasting trophy she might turn into a husband."

Lieberman even speculated on Chandra's sex life, saying, "Chandra probably did things in bed with Gary that she'd never done before and hadn't necessarily wanted to do [. . .] a realm of wild sex she'd never known. But she was also proving to him what a devoted love slave she could be and why he should marry her. She would have done anything he asked if it meant keeping him."

It seemed that any and all sources, anonymous or not, were fair game. To land exclusive interviews, journalists tracked down anyone who might at some point have crossed paths with Chandra. They had the means to pay sources and did not hide it.

Jakub Mosur, a friend of Chandra's from San Francisco State, remembers providing a sentence or two for the *San Francisco Examiner*. It was hard to turn them down because he sometimes collaborated with the paper as a photographer, and one of their journalists was a former professor of his. After his name was published, his phone rang nonstop. He recalls an interview with Fox News that was particularly uncomfortable. "They asked these really pointed, biased types of questions, trying to make a scandal . . . They wanted to make her look like a kind of very bad person, the victim but also partly responsible."

A few months later, Mosur was hired to shoot a press conference in front of the Levy home. It left a bitter taste in his mouth. But it's possible the *New York Post* took it a step further than anyone else. From May 17 onward, the tabloid published articles about Chandra daily, sometimes multiple times a day, often describing her as "the pretty brunette."

The first article claimed the police had found a framed picture of her and Condit in her apartment (not true). On July 13, the *New York Post* reported that Condit "was into massages" and "got his muscles soothed" at the same spa as Monica Lewinsky. On August 12, an astrologist weighed in on Levy and Condit's romantic compatibility. On September 6, the paper reported that Adrian Condit, Gary's father, assumed Chandra was dead, while his wife Jean believed the girl had staged her own disappearance to draw attention to herself. The Condit patriarch, a pastor, added, "Satan had a big-time role in this."

It became clear that the topic was simply unavoidable when Dan Rather—who was sixty-nine and an established newscaster by the summer of 2001, and who had, until this point, refused to get down in the mud with the other media outlets, boasting to *The New York Times* that he supported "decent" journalism—found himself tackling the case on his own show, *CBS Evening News,* as of July 18.

The Washington Post, which also tended to provide serious journalism, fully derailed when on July 29, it described Chandra as, "The dynamo with the size-2 body and size-12 ego [who] sometimes spoke of becoming a model."

On some level, perhaps the deluge of comments about Chandra's body can be attributed to the photo of her that was distributed and published throughout the country. The first shot—the one we will never forget, just as we will always remember JonBenét Ramsey's pageant shots—is an odd choice. In the photo, Chandra is posing in front of a marbled background, wearing high-waisted skinny jeans and a white tank top, with a seductive smile.

The photo is vaguely sensual because it was a glamour shot taken by a professional photographer when Chandra was building up a portfolio and toying with the idea of modeling. She was seventeen at the time. So, the photo her parents chose, the one published by every media outlet, was seven years old when Chandra went missing.

Michael Doyle recalls being surprised. "It was a very sexually charged photo. There was an exploitation of her sexuality, yes [by the media]. There is more sensitivity now, I think, with the use of pictures."

Chandra's parents hadn't given it a second thought. Susan recalls that she just wanted to quickly find a nice picture of her daughter. "I thought they were going to use just her face. I wasn't thinking that it was too sexual, sensual, or anything. I didn't really care about what people thought of the picture. I really just wanted information."

It didn't help that in this photo, Chandra looked a little like Monica Lewinsky. The round face, something about the smile, beautiful brown curls. Of course the press was going to compare the two young women, even without the photo, but it was a surprise when Rabbi Samuel M. Stahl, from Texas, dove into the fray.

His sermon made the rounds throughout the American Jewish community: "Monica and Chandra are examples of the spiritual deterioration marring segments of the American Jewish community. [. . .] Both families seem to have lost their moral compass. Monica told her mother about her affair with Bill Clinton in the Oval Office, but her mother never said she shouldn't behave like this. Chandra confided to her aunt about her ties with Condit. Instead of advising her to stay away from married men, her aunt gave her suggestions on how to win him. What about the embarrassment and shame that these two Jewish girls bring to all of us in the American Jewish community?"

For Chandra's loved ones, it was hard to witness this overexposure and barrage of snap judgments. Her friend Jennifer Baker, after putting up posters all over town and getting involved in events and press conferences, decided to lie low. Linda Zamsky, Chandra's aunt, had to live with a legion of journalists outside her home in Chesapeake City. One day, while she was soaking in the tub, they even stuck a TV microphone through the bathroom window.

And what about Susan Levy? The world seemed to be hell-bent on telling her that her daughter was a slut. She slept in Chandra's bed to feel close to her and tried to express her anger through painting. She felt that, at her core, everything shattered a little more with each passing day. And Bob, the inconsolable father, who couldn't stop himself from shouting in pain during interviews? And Adam, the little brother, just barely an adult, whose life would never be the same again? "Everyone had an opinion," sighs Susan, "but none of them really knew Chandra. All the BS that was written . . . We tried not to care. I tried not to internalize it."

Journalists blocked nearly the entire street on Chenault Drive. They parked themselves in lawn chairs, and watched for the slightest sign of life. Some of them weren't even professionals, just true crime fans who hoped that in scrutinizing the Levys, they could get a glimpse of the banality of evil.

When the phone rang in the Levy home, the callers were sometimes psychics offering to share their "visions" with Chandra's parents. One of these callers, Sylvia Browne, was as famous as she was controversial. She got her hands on Susan's number, called her, and claimed she was sure her daughter's body had been left in a swamp somewhere. Susan hung up on her.

Another psychic showed up at the door. This time, it was a friend of a friend, and the Levys felt they had to invite her in. In the family living room, they asked her, "If you're such a good psychic, where did Chandra sit at the table? Where is her bedroom?" She got it all wrong. And yet, the woman went on to claim she was the family's "personal psychic."

When TV stations crossed a line and aired reports on Chandra that were utterly demeaning, the Levys' lawyers would take the family out to dinner. Sometimes, on the way home, Susan would offer their leftovers to the vultures outside her door. She brought them hot coffee.

They had no regard for her feelings, little empathy for the people they watched all day, but was it really their fault? They didn't know Chandra, her Chandra. The girl her father loved with all his heart, the girl he watched grow up and build confidence as she began to draw an outline of the person she wanted to become. People don't have the capacity to feel what you feel. That's what Susan took away from all this.

3.
CONDIT COUNTRY

2001, RAYBURN HOUSE

In Gary Condit's office in Washington, DC, there were no photos of handshakes with the great leaders of the world or any pictures of his wife and two kids. There were only close-up shots of Condit himself. Referred to as "Mister Blow-Dry" on Capitol Hill, the man was fastidious about his appearance. As a teen, he had dreamed of looking like James Dean. Over time, his role model had morphed into John F. Kennedy. He was young, well established in his district, nicknamed "Condit Country," and he knew how to make friends in the Capitol on both sides of the aisle. In short, Gary Condit had his eye on the presidency.

THE WOMAN WHO VANISHED FROM DUPONT CIRCLE 65

Yet, unlike Kennedy, Condit was not from a privileged or political family. He was the son of a Baptist preacher from Oklahoma. Growing up in the Condit household, there was no drinking, no smoking, not even dancing. All three Condit sons worked the oil fields in the summer and were expected in church four times a week. Of course, young Gary did the exact opposite. As a rowdy teenager, his love of partying and fast cars repeatedly got him in trouble with the cops.

His wild years came to an end in high school, when he fell in love with Carolyn Berry, a well-behaved, petite blonde and the daughter of a respected middle-class business owner, and she convinced him to stop drinking. On January 18, 1967, at the age of eighteen, they said "I do" in a discreet ceremony without any guests. There are two likely reasons for this. First, Gary told city hall he was twenty-five to avoid having to ask for his father's permission to marry. Second, Carolyn would give birth to their first child exactly six months later, so the marriage was likely a bit rushed.

The couple moved to California right after Chad's birth, following Gary's parents. This took them farther away from Carolyn's parents, who disapproved of the union. A baby girl, Cadee, was born several years later.

Gary entered politics through his work to oppose the Vietnam War and, at twenty-six, he became the youngest mayor in the history of Ceres, a small city right next to Modesto. In 1989, when Tony Coelho, the district representative and the House majority whip, resigned in the wake of a financial scandal, Condit jumped on the occasion and, against all odds, won the vacant seat.

As it turned out, he was a natural politician. Comfortable in public, polite with old ladies, and charming, he quickly understood this little corner of California that was geographically close to major progressive cities but far removed ideologically. Inland, people mostly cared about agriculture, and that suited Condit, a conservative Democrat, just fine.

In 1994, he and others founded the "Blue Dogs," a group of Democrats aligned with Republicans. Condit, who was reelected six times, voted against the wars in Iraq and Kosovo, like all Democrats, but also bucked his party to vote in favor of the death penalty, mandatory prayer in schools, and releasing the identities of AIDS patients. In 1998, he vehemently condemned Bill Clinton's relationship with Monica Lewinsky.

In the spring of 2001, Condit must have regretted those words. This time, *he* was the one embroiled in a sex scandal—and a potential criminal investigation.

His life had seemed so perfect, but now, layer by layer, his lies were beginning to disintegrate, allowing the truth to show through. The congressman was not who he claimed to be.

After Linda Zamsky came forward and shared the details of his affair with Chandra, another mistress surfaced. This came as a surprise. Flight attendant Anne Marie Smith, aged thirty-nine, had been having an affair with Condit for almost a year. They'd first crossed paths on a flight from Washington to San Francisco and, since then, had been meeting in hotels and at his condominium in Adams Morgan.

Smith knew Condit was married and didn't ask him for anything. From the very beginning of their relationship, he'd made it clear that he would never leave Carolyn and confided that his wife was very ill. Smith understood it to be some kind of serious brain problem.

She hadn't really followed the news about Chandra Levy's disappearance, so it wasn't until May 17 that she connected the dots, when Condit called to say he was "in trouble" and might have to "disappear for a while." That night, Smith asked Condit if he'd actually had a relationship with the young intern, to which Condit responded that he "couldn't believe" she was asking him "these types of questions." Smith read between the lines, and when she looked into the Chandra Drama, she recognized the hallmarks of the strange relationship she'd had with Condit for the past year: the secrecy, the answering machine with the elevator music.

On June 1, concerned for her safety, Smith contacted the FBI. They were all ears. In fact, the FBI was already aware of her involvement in the story because, two weeks earlier, a few agents had heard from yet another one of Condit's mistresses.

Joleen Argentini had contacted the FBI as soon as she'd read about the affair between the missing Dupont Circle girl and Gary Condit. At first, she had refused to give them her name, so the agents called her "Janet." When she told them her story, it was clear why she'd want to remain anonymous.

In 1992, when Janet was a twenty-two-year-old student, she'd dated Mike Dayton, one of Condit's aides. One evening, the three of them had even had dinner together, but Janet promptly forgot about it. A year later, she and Dayton were no longer in a relationship when he asked if she could do him a favor. At the time, she was in school in Los Angeles, and Dayton was hoping she could give the congressman a ride to an event in town. Despite the twenty-two-year age gap, Janet and Condit started a relationship that would last three years.

During this time, he often paid for her flights to Washington so they could spend time together. After Janet graduated, Condit offered her a job in his office on Capitol Hill and had her live in his apartment. Like the other affairs, their relationship was all secrecy and subterfuge, especially since Janet had to lie to her colleagues. Condit was also a jealous and manipulative lover. When Janet broke down in tears at the office one day, upset over their unhealthy relationship, he made her promise to say she was just "sad about a breakup."

Eventually, Janet reached her limit when Cadee Condit came to town and the two women became friends. The guilt was overwhelming. She broke things off with Condit, quit her job, and moved back to the West Coast, where she went into advertising. But Condit wasn't ready to let go. Two weeks later, he flew to San Francisco to see Janet. In the end, the affair lasted for another year and a half, until Janet met her future husband and found the strength to leave Condit for good.

Again, Condit had to have the last word: Three years later, while visiting San Francisco, he pushed Janet to meet with him at a Starbucks. Sitting across the table, he looked her dead in the eye and criticized her new life, her new job, her new husband. He told her that soon, she'd grow tired of her husband and then she'd come crawling, she'd beg Condit to take her back. That was the last time they ever spoke.

Janet's story did not stay anonymously tucked away in FBI files. On July 10, a few hours before police searched his condominium in Adams Morgan, Condit was spotted by a witness who watched him walk up to a public garbage can and push a small package deep into the bin. Intrigued, the passerby took a look at the package. It was a box for a luxury watch, a TAG Heuer. Investigators were able to determine that Janet had given it to him more than seven years before. It's hard to understand how clumsily Condit went about trying to erase all traces of his mistresses from his life.

Now, in Washington, nearly everyone had their own story about Congressman Condit. But one person knew more than the rest. Vincent Flammini had been Condit's driver, friend, and bodyguard for nearly a decade. Ever since he was questioned by the FBI, Flammini had been having a field day with the media. According to him, Condit had been cheating on his wife since high school, had four separate phones to manage his affairs, told some of the women that his wife was seriously ill, and was obsessed with sex.

And Flammini knew Janet well. He had driven the couple all over San Francisco. He even claimed that his main job, in addition to the usual driver responsibilities, was to lie to Carolyn Condit. Although Flammini swore to anyone who would listen that he believed Condit was no assassin, just a fickle man, the congressman's reputation had become utterly unsalvageable. The tabloids smelled blood in the water.

Condit was a motorcycle buff and was known to ride a Harley-Davidson when he was back in his home state. It turned out he was also friends with some members of the Hells Angels in the area. Of course, this news sent the rumor mill into overdrive. Soon, the theories went a step further, suggesting Condit had "rough bondage sex" with other bikers, that he was gay or bisexual, depending on the rumors, and that predilection had something to do with Chandra's disappearance.

These new tales about his sex life stemmed from a statement made by Anne Marie Smith's lawyer, who claimed that her client had seen neckties knotted together underneath Condit's bed, "as if someone had been tied up." Smith reportedly also mentioned that he had specific sexual fantasies.

On July 23, the now defunct AheadNews.com reported that a cleaning person in the Adams Morgan building, who had been asked to clean the congressman's apartment "twice" between May 2 and May 5, had discovered a closet full of sex toys used for domination play. The *National Enquirer* reported that another Condit mistress had heard him say he had a "team" ready to deal with a body if needed.

And thus, like all criminal investigations involving an illicit affair, the Chandra Drama led to the inevitable question: Had Chandra died during sex play gone wrong? The question got the public all worked up. But no one would push this theory further than John LeBoutillier. He had briefly been a congressman and was on his way to becoming a full-fledged conspiracy theorist, when he wrote a 2001 *Newsmax* article entitled "Congressman Gary Condit: Gays, Bisexuals and Murder." The text wasn't online for long, as the site quickly took it down, fearing a lawsuit, but it was published just long enough to make its way, email by email, through Capitol Hill.

In the article, LeBoutillier laid out his theory, based on a story from an anonymous source to whom he attributed significant credit. He claimed Gary Condit had a habit of hiring prostitutes, with a preference for Caribbean men who were into motorcycles and leather. Condit had allegedly asked one of these men to pick Chandra up at her place on his motorcycle, then kill her, and disappear into his home country. LeBoutillier ended the article with "Buckle your seatbelts: Things are going to explode soon."

❖

This was simply too much for the good people of Modesto. Condit Country then turned against its own congressman. At the Fourth of July parade, protesters with placards demanded that Condit cooperate with the police to help find Chandra. In an editorial, *The Modesto Bee* officially withdrew its endorsement of Condit. The media pressure was so intense that the police had no choice but to take a closer look at the congressman.

After first questioning him discreetly at his home on May 15, then once again on June 22, investigators conducted a search of the Adams Morgan condominium on July 10. Condit and his lawyer, Lowell, were both present for the search, which yielded nothing.

Up until this point, Condit had not been particularly cooperative. Although he had submitted a DNA sample, as requested by investigators, he had refused to take a polygraph test at the police station, instead arranging to have a private test done with his lawyer and an examiner of his choosing. This made law enforcement furious, albeit powerless. Condit was not officially being charged with a crime, and therefore had no legal obligation to comply with their requests.

Over the month of July, however, his attitude began to change—if only a little. During his third interrogation, Condit finally admitted to having an affair with Chandra. Although the revelation was immediately leaked to the press, Condit never reiterated the statement publicly. But that didn't matter because the DNA he provided told the story for him when the police found his sperm on some of Chandra's underwear collected from her apartment. Strangely, that's the only fact in the entire investigation that didn't end up being leaked.

The police also asked Condit to provide a complete list of his whereabouts in late April and early May. This was his opportunity to present what he believed to be solid alibis. On April 29, 2001, he had attended a luncheon at the White House to celebrate the first hundred days of George W. Bush's presidency. He had just bucked his party to vote in favor of the president's budget plan.

In exchange, Condit had been granted a few minutes of President Bush's time to talk about the energy problems in his region and a promised meeting with Vice President Cheney, which did eventually happen on May 1, the day Chandra disappeared. It was held between 12:30 and 1:15 p.m., around the time Chandra logged off the internet. The vice president's office did not corroborate the timeline right away, likely in no hurry to have Cheney's name tied to this tawdry affair. Eventually, they did confirm that the meeting had occurred, although their schedules showed a slightly shorter conversation.

So what did Condit do next? His staff mentioned an appointment with a doctor, at about 5:00 p.m. or maybe it was at 6:00 p.m. But no one could say who the doctor was. Condit told investigators he remembered going back to his office afterward and possibly to the gym as well. Eventually, he gave them a list drawn up by his aides. It included an interview at Tryst Coffeehouse with an ABC journalist, who later said that the meeting had actually taken place on May 2, the following day. The truth in all this is that Condit was just getting his dates mixed up—on May 1, he had in fact spent the rest of the day in Congress, where he had voted twice. Then he'd spent the evening at home with his wife.

On July 26, FBI agent Brad Garrett, who had just been assigned to the case, asked to see Condit again, as a person close to Chandra. He didn't think the congressman was guilty—there was no clear evidence incriminating him—and wanted to go over the case from the beginning to try to understand Chandra's personality. Condit was cooperative and told Garrett that Chandra was a vegetarian, took vitamins, stayed away from drugs, and wasn't particularly interested in nice clothes and fashion. And that was about it.

By the time Garrett left the interview, he was fairly certain of one thing, based on the way the congressman talked about Chandra: Condit simply didn't care enough about Chandra to kill her. Still, it appeared he was one of the last people to have seen her, possibly *the* last person, and to have spoken to her before her disappearance. That's why, when Bob and Susan Levy flew back to DC for a second time at the end of June, they demanded that he meet with them.

This wasn't the first time the Levy parents were contacting Condit directly. When they were looking for their daughter on May 6, before even notifying the police, it was his number they'd seen on Chandra's phone bills. At first, they couldn't understand why the number never rang, why it just played a line of elevator music. Then, as they'd moved down the list of numbers, they'd come across the number for Gary Condit's congressional office.

Susan Levy had felt her stomach turn. Were her worst fears coming true? Contrary to what she'd initially told the press, Chandra's mother knew her daughter was

THE WOMAN WHO VANISHED FROM DUPONT CIRCLE 77

seeing Gary Condit. She knew because her instincts told her so. And because Modesto was a small town . . .

❖

It had started out as just a normal conversation, a few months before Chandra's disappearance. Susan Levy was aware that her daughter was dating someone in Washington, but she still didn't know who he was. That day, she was in the backyard feeding the horses and chatting with Otis Thomas, a local Pentecostal minister who sometimes picked up odd jobs as a gardener. "We were talking about our kids, and I told him Chandra was in DC. We were kind of worried about them," she recalls today.

Thomas was no stranger to worrying about his own daughter and confided that his daughter, who was now twenty-five, had been in a relationship with Condit when she was only eighteen.

"His daughter told him that Condit wanted her to come to parties with his friends [and] it was more than just a party, it was borderline prostitution," Susan recalls. When Thomas's daughter ended her relationship with Condit, she "was concerned for her safety." She'd been told to keep her mouth shut, and she left town, afraid.

Standing in the yard, Susan worried about her own daughter. What if Chandra's secret friend was, in fact, Condit, as she'd suspected? The man had to be married; otherwise, why bother with all the secrecy? He was probably old—what else could explain the fact that Chandra was suddenly listening to Frank Sinatra? And if he was from Modesto, it would make even more sense.

Susan called up Chandra and told her everything. At first, Chandra was surprised Susan had figured it out, then she told her mother to mind her own business. When they saw each other again for her birthday in mid-April, Chandra reassured Susan, saying she had talked to Condit about it, and he'd explained it all. Everything was OK.

But on May 6, Susan felt that everything was very much not OK. She and Bob looked up the Condit family's number in the phone book. They initially got Carolyn on the line, but Gary was quick to call back. Bob explained that his daughter had disappeared and asked if Condit had any information that could help. When Condit responded that he barely knew Chandra, Susan yanked the phone out of Bob's hands and asked point-blank whether he'd been having an affair with her daughter. Condit's answer was "no."

The meeting between Chandra's parents and her lover occurred on June 21, at the Jefferson Hotel. By this time, Bob and Susan knew for a fact that Condit had lied when they'd called his home a month and a half earlier. So what else could he be hiding? The interview was planned and conducted under the strict supervision of Condit's lawyer. Meanwhile, Susan had worked with their family lawyer, Billy Martin, to craft clear and concise questions they could ask the man she deemed to be suspect number one.

At the last minute, Bob pulled out. He didn't have the strength to go through with it, so Susan would be facing Condit alone. When she arrived, she refused to shake his hand. The ensuing meeting was both very brief and very intense. Susan barely had time to think that Condit didn't really look like Harrison Ford and wondered what her daughter had seen in him.

But that wasn't the issue at hand. Susan had questions to ask. And, especially, she wanted answers. When did you first meet Chandra? When was the last time you saw her? Do you have any information about where she is now? Susan Levy can barely recall what little Condit told her. He knew nothing. He was sorry. After just fifteen minutes, when they got up to leave, Condit asked Susan if he could give her a hug. "Absolutely not."

The pressure continued to build all summer long until it became unbearable. There were not enough sharks in the ocean to tear the public's attention away from the Chandra Levy and Gary Condit affair. Eventually, Condit's team told him what he was hoping he'd never hear: It was time to make a media appearance. He'd be interviewed by ABC's Connie Chung.

On August 23, 2001, nearly twenty-four million Americans tuned in. The interview was held in a small beige living room overlooking a garden. Anyone who watched it can tell you the following thirty minutes were painfully long. Americans were expecting an apology from a man who felt bad about cheating on his wife. Instead, Condit just beat around the bush. He repeatedly dodged Chung's questions, going on about his marriage, and alluding to "mistakes" he'd made over the years. He also denied hindering the investigation, even though the police chief had claimed quite the opposite at a recent press conference.

With mounting tension, Chung tightened the vise and kept the questions coming. It was the longest half hour of Gary Condit's life. And when it was finally over, his reputation was in even worse shape. Six days later, Marina Ein, Condit's PR person, resigned.

❖

On September 11, 2001, Bob and Susan Levy were about to fly to Chicago, to be interviewed on a TV show—*The Oprah Winfrey Show*. Afterward, they would fly to New York for *The Today Show*. But shortly after 9:00 a.m., the Levys heard a ruckus out front. They peeked through curtains that had been drawn for months and watched as dozens of journalists, who had long been parked in their driveway, packed up their things in a hurry. Within just a few minutes, the horde was gone. The only noise was now the squeal of tires as the trucks peeled out.

Meanwhile, the same thing was happening in front of Zamsky's home in Chesapeake City, and in front of Condit's apartment in Washington, DC.

At 8:46 that morning, the entire world came to a standstill. The Chandra Drama, the media frenzy, the Summer of the Shark, the rumors, the search—America as Americans knew it. That morning, American Airlines Flight 11 collided with the north tower of the World Trade Center. And thoughts of Chandra were obliterated by the smoke that billowed out from the towers, by the dust that stuck to the faces of New Yorkers, by the fire that raged in the heart of the nation.

In Washington, journalist Michael Doyle left the Pentagon and was walking home from work. It must have been about 10:00 a.m. when he turned around to look back at the Pentagon. American Airlines Flight 77 had just crashed into the west side of the building. Doyle watched as thick black smoke began to fill the clear sky. On the sidewalk, he bumped into one of Condit's press managers, Randy Groves, who was standing by his bike, stock-still, his face upturned. For a few seconds, they were silent. Then Groves turned to Doyle and said, "Today's Gary Condit's lucky day."

ROCK CREEK PARK

1.
THE WORLD AFTER 9/11

MAY 2002

Philip Palmer, a forty-three-year-old furniture maker from DC's wealthy suburbs, was walking his dog Paco in Rock Creek Park. On this day, America was a very different place than it had been eight months earlier. On the streets of DC, armed soldiers stood guard on every street corner, unsmiling. The air smelled of love and sulfur.

Love, because people had never looked at each other so intently. They'd never checked in with each other so often. There had never been so many marriage proposals, so many babies on the way, so many career changes. For Americans, 9/11 was a reminder that life is short.

Sulfur, because a state of siege had begun, and a war too. It was happening in a faraway place, but you could feel it all around. You could see it in the rising paranoia, in sidelong glances in the subway, and dogs sniffing passersby and luggage.

Studies have shown that a quarter of Americans were thinking about it, what happened on September 11, every day. And a quarter of DC residents were having trouble sleeping, torn between anger and fear. In this moment of uncertainty, patriotic feelings provided a kind of lifeline for a floundering people. More than 60 percent of Americans said they felt more patriotic then than before the attacks. There were flags and stickers everywhere.

But soon, the unity seen in the first few months would begin to crack. In the Oval Office, the hawks, a small group of neoconservative interventionists, were almost done convincing President Bush that a war in Iraq was necessary, in addition to the war already underway in Afghanistan.

Philip Palmer was quite familiar with Rock Creek Park. And while it looked like a regular urban park on a map, it was in fact a forest. Spanning 1,750 acres, the park featured winding walking paths, as well as roads, bridges, sports fields, a zoo, an amphitheater, and a golf course. It was a long stretch of green space that straddled a state line and highlighted the divide between social classes.

To the west, the park bumped up against affluent neighborhoods, embassies, and Georgetown University. To the south were museums and Capitol Hill. The eastern border was flanked by predominantly Black and Latino neighborhoods plagued by drug trafficking and rife with weapons.

When you stepped into Rock Creek Park through one of the many paths along the perimeter, silence could set in within a few seconds. And while two million visitors came to the park every year, you could quickly feel quite alone in there.

On May 22, 2002, that suited Philip Palmer just fine. He'd been collecting deer antlers and animal bones since he was a kid. So Palmer often wandered off trails to find remains when out walking the dog. Sometimes, he made his way down steep slopes, holding onto trees that would gently bend under his weight.

That morning, it was nearly 10:00 a.m. when he spotted a piece of red fabric in the distance. He didn't think much of it. A little farther down, Paco took off and ran into a small ravine. Palmer followed and noticed a rounded mass on the ground that looked like a turtle shell. As he bent down to get a closer look, he realized he was looking at a human skull.

His breathing became short and his pulse raced, but Palmer didn't want to mess this up. He threw Paco's blue leash over a branch by the skull, to mark the spot, then hung his sweatshirt from a tree higher up the hill. He scrambled across a creek and walked until he hit a road. Then, with a cell phone borrowed from a construction worker, Palmer called 9-1-1.

❖

In Modesto, Bob and Susan Levy answered Oprah's questions from their living room. Three weeks after the first anniversary of Chandra's disappearance, they were hoping to get people talking about the case again, as the story had come to a standstill after 9/11. At 8:30 a.m. California time, the interview had just ended when the phone rang. Susan picked up. The officer used the word "might." "*Might* be Chandra." Not "*is* Chandra," not "*There's a chance it could be* Chandra." He said "*might*." Susan collapsed in the hallway.

Meanwhile, Michael Doyle, the reporter for *The Modesto Bee*, jumped into a taxi bound for Rock Creek Park. This was exactly the way he'd imagined it would go down. Just a normal day, a day when he wasn't thinking about the Levy case at all. Just a regular day, then it fell into his lap.

When he got there, the press was already gathering. Pat Collins from NBC was on location too. Earlier that day, he'd been monitoring police radio chatter when he'd heard dispatchers call in an emergency—and they sounded stressed. For a reporter, this was the perfect combination. Units from several different departments were sent to the scene. Collins rushed over. Others joined him, and by the time Doyle got to the park, he saw the hallmarks of a serious case. The police chief was there, with his second-in-command, as well as all the detectives working the Levy case. A TV presenter pulled up in a limousine.

Was this what the world after 9/11 looked like? Doyle was surprised. In fact, he's still surprised to this day. "After 9/11, there was a discourse. We were gonna be a sober nation now, less seduced by these trivialities. There were more important things in the world. And then . . ." All it took was one dead body, and everything was back on track. Promises of sobriety went out the window. Even on May 22, when there was a suspected bomb threat on the Brooklyn Bridge, TV and radio stations covered nothing but the body found in Rock Creek Park.

Just before 3:00 p.m., the phone rang again at the Levy residence. Susan and Bob don't remember which of them picked up. It was Billy Martin. There was no more "might." The skeletal remains in the park were Chandra's.

❖

Chandra's skull was found somewhere between Broad Branch Road NW, which runs along the park, and Picnic Grove 18, on the Western Ridge Trail. From Broad Branch Road NW, you'd have to climb up a ravine to get to the crime scene, if you were brave and fit enough to claw your way through the dense woods. To access the site from the Western Ridge Trail, you'd have to abseil down a steep embankment, with a precipitous 45-degree gradient in some places.

About halfway between the road and the trail, near a tree, law enforcement found several bones, black panties turned inside out, a red bra, a cassette player, black leggings, also turned inside out and knotted at the ends, and a gray T-shirt with "Property of USC Athletics" printed on the front. A little higher, closer to the hiking trail, they spotted sunglasses. Scattered throughout the surrounding area were headphones and white Reeboks.

It was hard to tell the difference between what could be critical crime scene evidence and what might have just been garbage left behind by passersby or carried into the woods by the wind. There were pantyhose, a condom wrapper, beer cans, lipstick, and a Baskin-Robbins ice cream wrapper.

Dr. Jonathan Arden, the medical examiner for the Metropolitan Police Department, also known as the Metro PD or the DC police, left with the skull and was able to identify Chandra using her dental records.

The rest of his work would prove to be far more complex. Chandra's body had likely been there for almost thirteen months and was fully decomposed. The bones had been scattered throughout the area, likely moved by animals and the elements. On May 28, Dr. Arden announced that he was unable to determine the cause of death. There was no evidence of gunshot or stab wounds on the remains, and although the skull was fractured, it appeared that the fracture had occurred postmortem because the bone showed no discoloration due to blood.

Damage to the victim's hyoid, a small bone above the larynx, indicated that she was possibly strangled. However, the bone was not fractured. At a press conference, Dr. Arden acknowledged, "It's possible we will never know specifically how she died." It's also impossible to know if Chandra was sexually assaulted, or if she had consensual sex in the final hours before her death. No evidence—like hair, clothing fibers, or blood—was ever found.

In California, the Levy parents had Judy Smith, from the family's communications team, organize a memorial service at the Modesto City Hall. Bob and Susan wanted something simple. Flowers poured in from all around the world. At the entrance, large vases were filled with Chandra's beloved Reese's peanut butter cups. Her brother, Adam, stood up to say a few words, as did Paul Zamsky, Chandra's uncle, and Fran, her godmother. Bob and Susan entered through a side door to avoid the hundred or so eager journalists.

Without anyone noticing, Anne Marie Smith sat a few rows behind them. Condit's former mistress wanted to pay her respects to this young woman she had never met but to whom she now felt quite close.

The Levys would have to wait another year for DC investigators to release Chandra's remains. The burial was held at Lakewood Cemetery, seven miles outside Modesto. Chandra was laid to rest next to her paternal grandparents, and all three gravestones bear the same inscription: WE ARE NOT HERE. "Because none of them are really there, they're in our hearts," Bob whispered.

No one wanted to bring up that fateful day, but one question still haunted every person who had come to pay their respects to Chandra. Why, in July 2001, when three DC police sergeants, twenty-eight cadets, and dozens of dogs searched Rock Creek Park, had they not found her body? The answer is both sad and simple. DC police chief Charles H. Ramsey had ordered his men to search the park one hundred yards from the roads *and* the trails running through the park. But Commander Jack Barrett, tasked with leading the search, either did not hear or misunderstood the second part of the sentence. So his team canvassed the area within one hundred yards of only the roads. A year later, Chandra's body was found seventy-nine yards from a hiking trail.

And that is just the start of a long list of mistakes made by the police. The blunders began in the first days following Chandra's disappearance. After Bob's call, police officers went to the Newport building for the first time on May 6. They returned on May 7 and May 8. On May 10, they filed a report about their findings in the apartment.

But no one thought to ask for recordings from the building's surveillance cameras. And yet the Newport was a secure building, with a guard on duty 24-7 and thirteen cameras recording every person entering and leaving the building. All security tapes were overwritten after seven days, so on May 8, the May 1 recordings were erased. No one was ever able to watch them. What time had Chandra left her apartment? Did she look like she was in a hurry? Was she alone? What was she wearing? These questions will forever remain unanswered.

Another important point is that when law enforcement first entered Chandra's apartment, one sergeant decided to take a closer look at her computer and accidentally caused a hard drive crash. Now, no one could see her search history or read her emails. The computer had to be sent to the FBI, which hired a private lab to take care of it. So the computer data—a critical piece of evidence in cases like these—would not be recovered for two more months.

That's why the first search of Rock Creek Park didn't happen until July 2001, when the Metro Police Department finally learned that Chandra had been on several websites about the park and its trails. However, investigators initially focused only on one of the park buildings, the Klingle Mansion, built in the nineteenth century and long used as the park's administrative HQ. This is because Chandra had accessed the Rock Creek Park website via a *Washington Post* link that brought her to a page about the Klingle Mansion. Quite some time went by before someone realized the URL may not have been Chandra's intended landing page, but rather a home page she'd used to find a map of the park and its trails.

At one point, a small amount of DNA briefly gave investigators hope. It was found on Chandra's bra and was swiftly analyzed. But this turned out to be just another dead end when the DNA matched an employee on the forensics team who had accidentally touched the fabric.

When it came to this case, could law enforcement and the justice system really be trusted? As *The Washington Post* reported at the time, the Metropolitan Police Department was no shining example in the profession. In fact, it was notoriously one of the most corrupt in the country in the 1980s and 1990s. And it wasn't the most effective either. In 1999, just two years before Chandra's disappearance, two thirds of the city's murders had gone unsolved.

The morgue was in no better shape. Hundreds of bodies stored there had yet to be examined, paper case files were never digitized, the lab that analyzed samples had no ventilation, and unidentified skeletal remains sat abandoned in boxes.

As for Dr. Jonathan Arden, the man who performed Chandra's autopsy and stated he couldn't draw any conclusions from her bones, he was forced to resign from his position in 2003, when five of his own employees accused him of sexual harassment and toxic management practices. A five-month audit later determined that the morgue was unable to fulfill even its most basic duties.

The police were under immense pressure, and it didn't take long for them to start turning against each other. Jack Barrett, the man leading the Levy investigation, was not a fan of Police Chief Charles H. Ramsey and his second-in-command, Terrance W. Gainer. In 2001, Barrett had just left the FBI to start a career with DC's Metropolitan Police Department. He was used to tough investigations, after working drug trafficking cases and taking on organized crime, but he was unaccustomed to working with cops who blabbed to journalists.

Meanwhile, Ramsey and Gainer seemed to be holding daily news conferences. Since the beginning of the investigation, countless confidential details had been leaked to the press, and Barrett was beginning to run out of patience. Where were the leaks coming from? Who was talking to the press? This was unacceptable behavior. After a few months, Barrett asked his detectives not to share their latest discoveries with him, because when they did, he had to write a report for his bosses, and this new information inevitably would find its way to the press.

Gainer and Barrett also had different opinions about where the investigation was headed. While Gainer wanted to dig into the Condit lead, Barrett was hoping to broaden his horizons. The two prosecutors assigned to the case, Barbara Kittay and Heidi Pasichow, tended to agree with Gainer and urged investigators to focus on leads related to the congressman, ignoring the rest.

Kittay especially wanted to put pressure on Condit. When she interrogated Carolyn Condit, and later Gary Condit, with the police present, she was tough. A little too tough, as far as Barrett was concerned, because he was trying to maintain a line of communication with the Condit team.

Despite their different approaches, Kittay shared Barrett's aversion to leaks and made her stance known. When, just one day after the interrogation in which Condit admitted to the affair, the news was on the front page of *The Washington Post*, Kittay asked to be taken off the case.

Now the Levy family was starting to wonder . . . If they couldn't count on law enforcement, who could they turn to?

2.
PARALLEL INVESTIGATIONS

Joe McCann is quite familiar with the Metro PD. He worked there for thirty-one years, first as a homicide investigator and later as the head of the department. Even at the age of seventy, in his fleece sweater and plaid shirt, he still gives off a strong "don't fuck with me" energy. Maybe it's in the way he maintains a professional tone at all times or the way he bangs his metal ring on the table to emphasize his points.

McCann quit the police force in 1999, and by 2001, he was working as a private detective, sometimes collaborating with his former colleague Dwayne Stanton. In May, he got a call from Stanton, who'd just been asked to help with the Levy case. He'd been hired by the family's lawyer, Billy Martin, and everyone figured it couldn't hurt to have two detectives on the case. McCann immediately had his own theories about Chandra's disappearance. "I was an old homicide detective. When you get a missing person and you call me, I think murder." He accepted the job.

You'd think working with the local police force, where, until recently, all the investigators still called McCann "J. T.," would be smooth sailing. But you'd be wrong. McCann's presence on the case drove a wedge in the DC police force. Officers who, out of loyalty, kept him apprised of progress in the investigation were quickly reprimanded.

Things became even more strained when it turned out that the cops and the private detectives had opposing agendas. The police, facing an unrelenting barrage of public criticism for their blunders and mishandling of the case, were beginning to resent the media. And although McCann had also loathed reporters when he was the lead investigator with the Metro PD, he found himself approaching this new case with a different strategy. From then on, McCann would be contacting the press to provide information about the case, because Billy Martin had made it quite clear he wanted to keep the story at the top of the news cycle.

Quite early on in the process, he allowed McCann and Stanton to speak with Chandra's parents. This is how they found out about her relationship with Condit. They interviewed her friends and colleagues, walked in her footsteps. They also set up a dedicated tip line and put up a reward. This turned out to be both a good and a bad idea. Every day, more than a hundred calls came in, and there were only two of them to sort fact from fiction.

There were several obvious leads: Chandra could have been sexually assaulted; maybe she was mugged. And then there was Condit. Sure, he didn't seem like the type of guy who shot people, but would he have been capable of ordering a hit on his girlfriend? To be determined.

The detectives were looking for a motive. Was she a gambler? Had she been involved in some kind of criminal activity? No. "Domestic murder," which at the time was not yet referred to as "femicide," was starting to look like a possibility. Maybe even a probability. After all, Gary Condit may have been a congressman, but he was still "the boyfriend."

One night, the detectives were hanging around the office after hours when the tip line lit up. A man was claiming he had information. He wouldn't tell them his name or where he was calling from, just that he'd been hired by the Hells Angels to dispose of Chandra Levy's body after an illegal abortion gone wrong.

At this point, McCann had heard it all and figured the story wasn't any wackier than the rest. Everyone knew about Condit's ties to the Hells Angels, and ever since Sven Jones had talked about Chandra's "female problem," rumors about a pregnancy had been gaining traction. But the informant told them he didn't want their reward. This, of course, only added to his credibility. Eventually, the informant caved and gave them his name, as well as a California address.

McCann and Stanton jumped into a taxi and rushed to the airport. En route, McCann got a call from a police investigator looking to discuss a potential lead, but the detective told him it would have to wait until he got back from California. When they met the informant in a hotel lobby, he was nervous and said he was afraid the Hells Angels would take him out if they got wind of his chat with the detectives. His story was the same as the one he'd told them over the phone. Someone had called him and promised him a lot of money. All he had to do was put Chandra's body in his car, then drive out to the Nevada desert and bury her. He didn't even know who she was.

But once they were out in the desert together, the informant couldn't remember exactly where he'd left the body. McCann and Stanton gave him time to collect himself and suggested meeting up again the next day. They piled back into the car and drove around the city. It was dark out, and they were in a deserted industrial area when McCann noticed they were being tailed by another vehicle. There were a few parked trucks between them, but the detective could make out headlights on the other side. When he sped up, the other vehicle sped up too. When he made a turn, it followed. After some time, McCann managed to lose the other car and dropped off the witness, now more agitated than ever, at his trailer park.

The next day, McCann and Stanton drove to Modesto to see Chandra's parents and talk to some of their friends. One thing was now clear to them: The pregnancy and abortion lead was highly unlikely. Chandra's parents didn't know if she was still taking birth control pills, but her father had given her a prescription for them years earlier. Everyone told them that Chandra would have been happy to find out she was pregnant, and that, although she was pro-choice, she would never have agreed to an abortion for herself. But could she have been forced into it? Possibly.

But Linda Zamsky remembered that during the Passover visit, Chandra had needed to borrow a few tampons. If she'd been on her period, how could she have been pregnant and already aware of it just three weeks later, at the time of her disappearance?

A few other details were bugging McCann too. If the informant had been paid so much money, why was the guy still living in a shabby trailer? And why was he talking? Who would accept money to bury a young woman without asking any questions and then suddenly feel bad for her parents?

The detectives circled back to talk to their witness, and Stanton stayed in the car while McCann knocked at the plastic door. What followed was a heated altercation. McCann shouted. The informant shouted. McCann said he'd better show him the money—if it was even real. The man pulled a bag full of banknotes out from under a table. Ten thousand dollars. He pulled out a gun too and pointed it at McCann.

Gingerly, McCann turned around and put his hand on the door handle, every motion deliberate. He slowly walked back to the car. McCann was unarmed. All he could do was keep his cool. Once he was finally in the car, the detectives sped off. What had happened?

"Remember the phone call from the police?" he asks, as if he's lining up to tell a good joke on stage. "That guy stabbed me in the back. He went to the media, the

Enquirer, and said, 'Hey, the Levy investigator is flying to California.' So the *Enquirer* followed us, they eventually found the guy, I don't know how, and gave him the $10,000 for the story. That guy was [. . .] a professional bullshit artist. He had been on TV on a well-known talk show, pretended to be a fire investigator . . . He's been locked up now."

Stanton and McCann went on to follow many leads like this one—until the body was discovered in May 2002. For several weeks, the perimeter was cordoned off by the police. Once the crime scene was released, McCann and Stanton headed for Rock Creek Park, armed with a shovel and two rakes. They wanted to pore over the area themselves and make sure all evidence had been collected. It took them only a half hour of raking to uncover a bone. They looked at each other, incredulous. The bone was white, with slight bite marks, and was about twelve inches long. It was hard to miss.

McCann pulled out his phone and called his former employer, the Metro PD. An officer came by to collect the evidence, saying it was probably just an animal bone. Except it wasn't—it was Chandra's left tibia. So, the police returned and searched the area for nineteen more days. This time around, they found bones from her hands, foot and back, one bone from her heel, and—most embarrassingly—a femur, the largest bone of the human body.

On the day the tibia was discovered, McCann and Stanton were asked to drop by the station for an interview. This was standard police procedure, so they complied. McCann was about to leave when an officer, clearly embarrassed, instructed him to sit back down. His bosses wanted him to take a polygraph test.

McCann was insulted. "Basically, I said 'fuck you' and I left." Afterward, he says the relationship became even more strained, and, even years after the Chandra Levy case, the Metro PD never missed an opportunity to make life difficult for both McCann and Stanton. Much water has flowed under the bridge since then, but McCann is still tight-lipped about it.

Today, he is sure of one thing though. It's an instinct, really, call it a gut feeling... Sometimes the first suspect is still suspect number one.

3.
UNANSWERED QUESTIONS

Did the discovery of Chandra's body prove that Condit was innocent? When the news of her death spread across the country, Condit was no longer a member of Congress. He had not been reelected in March 2002, after a painful campaign in which journalists were more interested in finding out where he had buried his mistress's body than hearing about his political platform.

A few weeks before his election defeat, he had told a reporter from *The New York Times* about a Michael Mann film he'd just seen, on Muhammad Ali. "Everything had turned on him," Condit reflected, attempting to establish a risky comparison. "He stood up for principle, and the country was going the other way. They caught up with him, eventually [. . .] and now look at what we think of Ali."

Could Condit be the perfect example of how a national thirst for blood, sex, and scandals can lead to innocent lives being sacrificed on the altar of sensationalism and ratings? Twenty years from now, will he be remembered as a victim? Or as the person responsible for Chandra's death?

It's anyone's guess. The fact that her body was found in a park suggests she was assaulted, perhaps in an attempted mugging gone wrong, or maybe she was sexually assaulted. The knots in the leggings suggest the pants were used to tie her up. But why tie her up? To rape her, or rob her, or for consensual sex play? Unless the pants were used to move her body? There's no way to know for sure.

And the most basic question is still unanswered: What was she doing in Rock Creek Park? Journalists initially wrote that she was out jogging, based on statements from "anonymous sources." Her clothes could also suggest this was her intention. She wore leggings, sneakers, a "Property of USC Athletics" T-shirt, and had a Walkman with her. But are the clothes enough evidence to make this assumption? Leggings aren't necessarily sportswear, especially in the US, where people tend to wear them as everyday pants. In many Levy family home videos, Chandra is wearing leggings and a big sweater.

The police stated that they found her workout shoes in her apartment. Did this mean she had multiple pairs? Or did she use the Reeboks, found in the park, as nonathletic footwear? And why bring lipstick on a jog? All of Chandra's friends and family members have maintained that she never ran outside, instead keeping to treadmills in the comfort and safety of her gym.

Sven Jones, Jennifer Baker, Susan Levy, and Linda Zamsky have all adamantly said that Chandra would *never* have gone for a run in the park. She didn't like it, and the place spooked her. Chandra was simply not the type to venture into risky places. She was the kind of person who walked around with a can of pepper spray in her purse and bugged her girlfriends to do the same. In fact, she was so cautious that when the landlord once dropped by to pick up an item he'd forgotten at her place, she wouldn't let him in. Instead, she closed the door while retrieving the item. So, it's hard to picture her heading off alone in this massive park, driven by a sudden urge to jog on trails that even experienced hikers find challenging.

But according to Chandra's browser history, there's no question she did look up a map of the park. Is it possible, then, that she was on her way to see someone who had suggested they meet there? The police never figured out how Chandra got from her home to the park. She hadn't used her Metro card, she'd left her credit card in her apartment, and none of the city's taxi companies reported charging her as a client. Could she have shared a cab with someone else? Had she gotten a ride in a car or on a motorcycle? Chandra could very well have walked to the park, but it would have taken her an hour and twenty minutes on an 80°F afternoon.

What we do know for sure is that Chandra left behind all her belongings, even her cell phone, which she always had on her. She took her Walkman and keys, but the keys were never found. Some people, like Joe McCann, assume she went out in a hurry, given the state of her apartment. She didn't take a second to put on her necklace, the one she always put back on as soon as she stepped out of the shower.

In the entrance, on the floor, the police found a clean comforter. Yet McCann claims that, according to all the people he questioned, Chandra was very tidy, not really the type to leave a comforter out on the floor for hours. Maybe Chandra had been washing the comforter when someone called suggesting they meet up. She could have quickly gone to the laundry room at the end of the hall and brought it back to the apartment before heading out in a hurry.

On the kitchen counter was a bag of dirty laundry containing a pair of underwear that would later turn out to have Gary Condit's DNA on it. Maybe she hadn't had enough time to get a second load started before leaving? And what if there hadn't been a call at all? What if the date had been set the day before, or the day before that?

On the morning of May 1, Chandra had also checked out the Baskin-Robbins website to see a map of their store locations. There was one franchise near Rock Creek Park, but the cops interviewed the store manager, and, according to him, none of the employees remembered seeing Chandra. It was hot out, though, and the store had been busy that day. The fact that a Baskin-Robbins ice cream wrapper was found in one of the park garbage cans could be just a coincidence. Or maybe Chandra had bought a pint to share with someone in the park.

According to the press, this bit of trash was sent to the FBI. It's one of many pieces of evidence that were collected by the police but that no one can say for sure were ever analyzed.

Another mystery is whether the location in which the body was found, isolated and relatively inaccessible, is in fact the scene of the crime. The spot is flanked by a road and a trail. Someone could easily have parked on Ridge Road NW, near Picnic Grove 18, and dumped Chandra's body into the ravine, then driven off. Furthermore, the police never stated whether Chandra's DNA was found in the surrounding soil, and they never provided any evidence that her body had in fact decomposed in that spot.

To the people who are sure Condit did it, one fact stands out. Wasn't he the only person Chandra went out to meet without carrying ID? When the police searched her apartment, they found two messages from the congressman on her answering machine. In the first one, he said, "It's eleven forty-five, I'm sorry, I've been tied up for the last few days, but you already know that. Give me a rundown on kind of what your schedule is. Things are looking pretty good for me today anyway. Bye." The message was dated May 3. Condit's wife had just left DC.

A little later that same day, he left a second message. "It's around six thirty. I haven't heard from you. Maybe you're out of the country or something. Anyway, give me a call if you get this message. Bye."

Chandra had been missing for two days. Was Condit actually trying to reach her, or were these messages just an attempt to build an alibi? If the latter were true, it was a risky bet. If he was trying to avoid being connected to the case, wouldn't he have opted to keep his ties with the victim hidden for a little longer?

As the months went by, every lead seemed to dry up. The Metro PD didn't have enough evidence to charge Condit, and they had too little to focus on another suspect. Like so many before it, Chandra Levy's disappearance was slowly becoming a cold case.

❖

In another part of the city, at the same time, one woman was suffering through sleepless nights. Ever since Chandra's body had been found, Halle Shilling couldn't stop thinking about it. About her attacker's dark eyes. The glint of the small knife in his hand. She remembered feeling something primal click in her head when she decided she wouldn't let him kill her. She remembered a voice shouting "No, no, no!" and then realizing it was her own voice. She remembered how, in a flash, lessons from an old self-defense class had come to her, and she'd dug her nails into her attacker's mouth. She remembered the sound of his footsteps speeding up as he fled.

The attack occurred on May 14, 2001, in Rock Creek Park. In the spring of 2002, Halle Shilling was a thirty-one-year-old college professor. Her attacker had been in prison for months and had recently been handed a ten-year sentence. But she couldn't stop watching the footage, aired over and over, of the police collecting Chandra Levy's bones. That could have been her. Could the attacker have assaulted her just a few days after killing Chandra? She waited for the police to call. But the call never came.

Amber Fitzgerald didn't know Halle Shilling, but she too was having trouble sleeping. A young lawyer with long blonde hair, she was replaying a scene in her head, nonstop.

In May 2001, she had crossed paths with a man while out jogging in the park. Her boyfriend was faster than her, so he was far ahead, and she found herself alone somewhere along one of the trails in the west end of the park. She sensed someone was watching her, and locked eyes with a man standing in the underbrush. He was about five feet, six inches tall, with dark eyes and a hood pulled down over his head. He seemed to be coming toward her.

Fitzgerald put her head down and picked up the pace. She lost sight of the man and, then, as if in a nightmare, he was suddenly in front of her, motionless and blocking her way. Fitzgerald was terrified. She ran as fast as she could in the opposite direction. At the time, it didn't occur to her to report the incident. Nothing had actually happened, so what would she have told the cops?

But she had since checked several times, comparing the dates in her calendar with those of her ex-boyfriend. It had definitely been May 1, 2001. Wasn't that the day the intern was supposed to have gone missing? Hadn't she been found in the same park?

In 2003, unable to wipe this coincidence from her mind, Fitzgerald finally contacted the police. The officers nodded and thanked her. And they never called her back.

THE MAN IN THE PARK

1.
WHO KILLED CHANDRA LEVY?

Every trial is a bubble. A world apart, with its own characters, its own hierarchy and plot twists. It is suspended in time, separate from society. Michael Doyle has compared it to a political campaign or a sports season. For those involved, nothing exists beyond the bubble.

The year was 2010. The H. Carl Moultrie Courthouse—in Washington's Golden Triangle, a place Chandra had dreamed of, between the White House and the Capitol and just a half mile from her former office—was a hive of activity. It was October 25, and a trial was about to begin for the man accused of murdering Chandra Levy.

Michael Doyle watched as journalists from elsewhere came in droves to see the show. *He* had been here since the very first minute of the investigation. On this morning, as he would for many mornings to come, Doyle flashed his badge and went through security with a small group of journalists assigned to the case. He sat in the second row, on the left, in the space set aside for the press. Since he was a nice guy, Doyle was happy to answer questions from newcomers. He pointed out the people in the room.

The distinguished gentleman with the gray hair was Judge Gerald Fisher, and next to him, the young forty-four-year-old with a big laugh was Amanda Haines, the prosecutor. She was charismatic and warm, and everyone liked her. By her side was Fernando Campoamor, her partner. He liked to fly planes in his spare time. On the other side of the room, the small woman who barely ever smiled was the defense attorney, i.e., Amanda Haines's rival. Her name was Santha Sonenberg. At her table was Maria Hawilo, a little younger, in her thirties.

In the second row, the woman writing in a notepad was Susan Levy, Chandra's mother. The judge gave her permission to attend the entire trial. And there, of course, with the beige jacket, his tattoos hidden by a turtleneck—he seemed to wear a different one every day, so the reporters had begun to joke, calling it "the collection"—that was the defendant: Ingmar Guandique.

THE MAN IN THE PARK 119

Sari Horwitz and Scott Higham needed no such introduction. The Pulitzer Prize–winning journalists from *The Washington Post* were shaking hands with people in the courtroom halls. They'd literally written the book on the case, *Finding Chandra: A True Washington Murder Mystery*, published six months earlier. Now here they were, *hugging* Susan Levy. They felt at home at this trial and, in fact, it was partly thanks to them that it was happening at all.

In 2007, when everyone had stopped talking about the story, the editors of *The Washington Post* had asked Sari Horwitz to revisit the case. She didn't need to be asked twice. Horwitz was quite familiar with the Chandra Levy case, as she had been working on it when the story exploded. Then, in 2002, she was pursuing a serious lead when snipers began shooting random people on the streets of Washington, DC. So she'd been moved to this new investigation, eventually leading to the arrest of John Allen Muhammad and Lee Boyd Malvo, who were charged with killing ten people over a three-week period in October 2002.

But she never stopped being obsessed with the Chandra case. In the years that followed, Horwitz kept a copy of the "Missing" poster of Chandra pinned up at her desk. In 2007, when she was assigned to the case again, the first thing she did was call back the source who had given her that promising lead five years earlier. That person, who has remained anonymous to this day, met with her for months, in cars, parks, and restaurants. Each time, Horwitz left with confidential documents that she opened only once she was back in her office.

After carrying out a yearlong investigation with her colleague Scott Higham, they published "Who Killed Chandra Levy?" a series of articles featured on the front page of *The Washington Post* for thirteen days in a row, in the summer of 2008. They claimed the police had conducted a botched investigation and missed the real murderer. They claimed his name was Ingmar Guandique.

❖

Ingmar Guandique was an undocumented Salvadoran man who had been in police custody the entire time. In 2001, at the age of twenty, he'd gone to jail for assaulting Halle Shilling on May 14, 2001, and for another assault that occurred on July 1 of the same year.

Christy Wiegand, a twenty-six-year-old lawyer, was jogging in the park that Sunday afternoon when she ran by a man sitting on a curb in the parking lot. When he began to follow her, she didn't stop running, but pressed

THE MAN IN THE PARK

the pause button on her Walkman. A few seconds later, she felt someone grab her from behind.

The attacker held a knife to her throat and covered her mouth with his other hand. Then he dragged her toward the woods and a steep slope. She fought him off, as they rolled down into a small ravine. Within seconds, Wiegand felt isolated, far from help. Here, no one could hear her, no one could see her. She screamed and continued to fend off the stranger. She was taller than him, and eventually he grew tired and ran away. Wiegand hurried back up the hill and called the park police. Forty-five minutes later, Ingmar Guandique was arrested by two park police officers on a street near Rock Creek Park.

Now, in February 2002, he was on trial for the two assaults, facing thirteen years for each crime, twenty-six in total. But before Judge Noël Anketell Kramer could hand down a sentence, prosecutor Kristina Ament asked to speak with her. She approached the judge's bench.

Ament quietly explained that, well, it was kind of absurd, and highly confidential, but she felt obliged to point out that Ingmar Guandique's name had come up in the Chandra Levy case. It turned out that five months before the hearing, in September 2001, the police got wind of a confession that Guandique had allegedly made to a fellow inmate. Apparently, he'd said that Condit paid him $25,000 to kill Chandra Levy and leave her body to rot in Rock Creek Park.

At the time, the park had been canvassed just a month and a half prior, and the police had found nothing. Investigators were still focused on the congressman lead, but the idea that he might have flagged down a stranger in the Adams Morgan neighborhood to then hand him a picture of a young woman and ask him to kill her for money . . . Well, it sounded ludicrous. However, it was the first time investigators were hearing about this man who'd attacked two women shortly after Chandra's disappearance.

Two detectives had been sent out to interrogate him in prison. Guandique denied any involvement in the case, claiming he had only ever seen Chandra on TV. The investigators had both Guandique and the informant take a polygraph test. Since both men were Spanish speakers and not fluent in English, an interpreter was called in, even though the presence of an interpreter was known to affect polygraph test results. The inmate failed the test and Guandique's results were inconclusive, but the person administering the tests chose to write that Guandique was telling the truth.

Now, Guandique was before Judge Kramer, and Ament wanted to stress that her client, the defendant, had been cooperative—he didn't have to agree to undergo a polygraph test. She added that Guandique had only sought to rob his victims so he could afford to pay his rent, as he was undocumented and sometimes struggled to find work under the table. The judge brushed aside any mention of the Chandra Levy case, deeming it "a satellite issue."

After hearing testimonies from Shilling and Wiegand, she also seemed to accept both women's claims that they were sure Guandique intended to rape or kill them and that the attacks were absolutely about more than stealing a Walkman or jewelry. Guandique didn't even look at the impressive engagement ring Wiegand had been wearing on the day of the attack. On February 2, 2002, Judge Kramer sentenced Ingmar Guandique to ten years in prison for the two assaults.

The *Washington Post* series written by Horwitz and Higham later revealed that more facts and evidence had been dismissed. Even after Chandra's body was found in Rock Creek Park, the police didn't look for potential ties to other assaults in the area. No one interviewed Halle Shilling and Christy Wiegand until 2008.

Another year went by, after Guandique's interrogation, before the police even remembered he existed. But one man had not forgotten. His name is Joe Green. With thirty years' experience under his belt, Green was one of the oldest park police officers, and he was the first to interrogate Ingmar Guandique.

After his arrest for the assault of Christy Wiegand, Guandique had spent the night in a cell in the small Rock Creek Park police station. It was 1:00 a.m. when Green, his colleague, and an interpreter stepped into the tiny room. Green managed to get Guandique to confess to the two assaults. Then, striking while the iron was hot, and since Chandra Levy was absolutely everywhere in Washington at this point, Green showed Guandique a photo of Chandra and asked if he'd ever seen her around. Guandique said yes. Green asked if he thought she was pretty. Guandique said yes. He said he had only seen her once, then never again. Green did not include these two questions in his report. In July 2001, he figured it was irrelevant.

❖

When the *Washington Post* articles entitled "Who Killed Chandra Levy?" came out in 2008, they brought the story—and perhaps even the case itself—back to life. No series published by a newspaper had ever been so widely read, celebrated, and criticized. While some people vilified the police for their mistakes and negligence, others were outraged that the paper would spend so much time and energy on the murder of a single woman when thousands of others had died since.

The DC police force wasn't particularly fond of the revelations either. At every opportunity, they were quick to point out that they had reopened the case before the *Washington Post* articles came out. In 2006, Police Chief Charles H. Ramsey had been replaced by Cathy L. Lanier, who assigned new detectives to the case. According to them, this new investigation—and no other factors—had led to the indictment of Ingmar Guandique in March 2009.

Still, Amanda Haines did not invite the police to attend the trial. When the proceedings began on October 25, 2010, she did admit, in her opening statement, that the investigation had been hindered by many failures and that the police had been "distracted by the romantic entanglement" between the young intern and the congressman. She went on, saying, "This is also a case about the secrets of a man named Gary Condit. He was having an affair with Chandra Levy, but it has nothing to do with the murder of Chandra Levy." And thus, she set the tone for the trial.

2.
CONFLICTING STORIES

For the people confined to the space–time of the Carl Moultrie Courthouse in October and November 2010, every day was much the same. At 11:00 a.m., during the fifteen-minute recess, journalists would spill out into the halls and furiously type on computers they weren't allowed to use in the courtroom. Some were already on Twitter, others posted on blogs and published at least one article per day for their newspaper. At 1:00 p.m., they stopped for lunch. At 4:00 p.m., they got another fifteen-minute break, published another blog post.

Michael Doyle wrote that daily news was now a thing of the past, ushering in an era of hourly news updates. On day one, Doyle wrote no fewer than five articles. He

THE MAN IN THE PARK

described the witnesses who took the stand: a park police officer, Halle Shilling, Amber Fitzgerald—who eventually got a call back from the police after her 2003 deposition—and Fitzgerald's ex-boyfriend.

Shilling was now thirty-nine years old and a mother of three, but her story hadn't changed in nine years. Deep down, she knew that day wasn't just about a Walkman—she'd been fighting for her life. A few tears rolled down her cheeks; she seemed angry.

Amber Fitzgerald made a different impression in court. She wasn't sure if the man she'd seen in Rock Creek Park on May 1, 2001, the man who had seemed so threatening, was actually Ingmar Guandique. But she did remember the date because she'd told her boyfriend about it when they'd had dinner together that night at an Italian restaurant in the Adams Morgan neighborhood.

Her ex-boyfriend was called to the stand, but his testimony only made matters worse. He referred to a jarringly detailed planner he'd kept since 2001. And although he did not recall Fitzgerald telling him about her scare in the park on May 1, he was able to confirm they'd eaten together that evening at Cafe Paradiso, that they'd likely had an argument because he'd added a sad face in his calendar, and that the disagreement was probably short-lived because she'd later spent the night at his place.

The couple also had met for dinner the following evening. The ex-boyfriend's meticulous note-taking, verging on obsessive, added an element of absurdity to the story and detracted from the gravity of Halle Shilling's powerful testimony. It was a major blow to the prosecution. But that's what trials are—an impression, an organic mood that each actor shapes and colors, and it can evaporate in a heartbeat.

On November 11, Ingmar Guandique officially decided not to testify in his own defense, as this meant he would avoid being cross-examined by Amanda Haines. During the four weeks of his trial, the twenty-nine-year-old Salvadoran thus remained silent. Yet he could have told the court about his own childhood tragedies, how his father had been assassinated before he was even born, killed by guerrillas in the Salvadoran civil war between anti-communists, backed by the Reagan administration and Cuban-backed rebels. To terrorize the local peasants, who needed no further reason to be afraid, his father's body had been thrown out of a pickup truck along a dusty country road.

Guandique could have told the court about the extreme poverty he experienced, the ramshackle home with a dilapidated roof he'd grown up in along with his six siblings. He could have told the court about the violence that surrounded him, ubiquitous, both at home and outside the home, and about how he quit school at twelve and worked in the fields. It was either that or join a gang. In the end, he did both, later becoming a member of MS-13, a Salvadoran gang based in the United States.

Guandique knew his family was counting on him to earn money, so he figured he'd rather try his luck in America instead of staying out in the countryside just waiting to end up like his father. A family friend lent him $5,000 to pay a coyote, and on January 13, 2000, Guandique was smuggled into Texas. He then took a bus from Houston to Washington, DC, where his half brother lived. While the nation's capital was supporting anti-communist factions in El Salvador, it was unwittingly welcoming hundreds of thousands of Salvadorans, illegal immigrants fleeing violence and weapons supplied by the United States.

Guandique worked in construction and sent money home to his family and to a girlfriend who was expecting his child. In the fall of 2000, while Chandra was getting to know Gary Condit, Ingmar Guandique was also falling for someone. Only a few miles stood between the two love stories—just the width of a park. Iris Portillo was twenty years old and baby-faced, and the couple enjoyed going out for picnics in Rock Creek Park.

But the relationship was short-lived. Guandique spoke little English and was tired of getting up at dawn in the hope that a site manager would hand him a meager wage. He didn't understand this country and couldn't bear the weight of this tragic destiny that had dogged him since birth. He started drinking, just cheap beers, and dabbling in drugs when he had enough money to buy them.

Now when he hung around Rock Creek Park, he wasn't smiling at Iris anymore. He was pissed, mad at the world. Guandique got himself a knife, "for self-defense," and began roaming the park with his hoodie on, watching wealthy women jog by, their perfect hair bouncing as they ran. Everything seemed so easy for them. He'd approach them and pounce, to steal a Walkman and some jewelry, or to wrest a little power from them as he caught a glimpse of fear in their eyes. What had gone through his mind when, on May 1, he saw Chandra Levy in her gray T-shirt? Or had he even seen her at all?

Prosecutor Amanda Haines had her own version of the story. It was simple: Ingmar Guandique was depressed, he was addicted to drugs and alcohol, and he needed money and power. To get what he needed, he followed women into Rock Creek Park, then jumped them with an intent to rape. On May 1, 2001, he was prowling around his usual haunts when he saw Chandra. He attacked her, raped her—or at least tried to—and then killed her.

To tell this story, Haines called on several witnesses. On October 27, Iris Portillo and Sheila Phillips Cruz were up. The defendant's ex-girlfriend took the stand wearing jeans and a black jacket. She was four feet, eleven inches tall, with hair down to her waist. She had ended things with Guandique when he was arrested in July 2001 but still visited him in prison from time to time, explaining that "he had no one else."

But Portillo had not forgotten the violence she sometimes experienced at his hands. Like Guandique, Portillo had a boyfriend back home, to whom she sent money. And Guandique was jealous. He hit her a few times because of it, and for other reasons. Portillo had trouble recalling dates, but she remembered that once or twice, he came home with scratches on his chest and said he'd been robbed. When? Portillo couldn't remember.

Sheila Phillips Cruz was a little more precise. She was the building manager where Guandique lived in 2000.

He'd stayed at her place a few times after arguments with Portillo. The first time was around mid-April, she said. The second time—this she remembered well—was in the first week of May. He had scratches on his face and a fat lip. Phillips Cruz never asked him what happened.

We also know Guandique didn't go to work on May 1, the day Chandra Levy disappeared. A few weeks later, a workman told Phillips Cruz that he'd found a pile of Guandique's clothes in a plastic bag at his old apartment. The workman threw it all out.

Michael Doyle later reported that Iris Portillo was not a great witness. Sheila Phillips Cruz didn't fare much better. She provided a few intriguing details, but nothing that significantly changed the atmosphere in the courtroom. There were no sparks. If the jury was to believe Amanda Haines's story beyond a reasonable doubt, they were going to need more, much more.

To this day, Doyle is still surprised. Compared to the madness of the case, he thought the trial "was pretty boring." The first week was over, and it was unclear which way things would go. But on the following Monday, the trial took a drastic turn. That day, it became evident that the prosecutor's case was based on a single witness, a man named Armando Morales.

THE MAN IN THE PARK

There are photos of Morales going back long before the 2010 trial, when he was a gang member with a shaved head and prominent tattoos. In photos taken recently, he's a small, round-faced man with a mustache, eyebrows going gray, looking almost jolly. The real Armando Morales lies somewhere between these two depictions.

In the hierarchy of the trial, he should have been at the very bottom. He was just a jailhouse snitch. Yet there he was, at the very top. On Monday morning, this former gang member, who'd been incarcerated since 1997 for drug trafficking, took the stand wearing the standard-issue orange prison jumpsuit. His feet and wrists were cuffed, his head shaved.

Morales had joined a gang in California when he was twelve years old. Since then, he'd known nothing but violence and settling scores. During his twenty-one-year sentence, Morales had spent time in several federal prisons. In 2006, he was transferred to Big Sandy, Kentucky, where he shared a cell with Ingmar Guandique for six weeks. Morales was twenty years older than Guandique.

Both men belonged to allied gangs, and they spent twenty-two hours a day in the same cell. So they talked. Guandique told his cellmate he used to hide in the bushes and attack women in Rock Creek Park so he could rob them. Sometimes he also broke into cars in the neighborhood. Then one day, Guandique seemed particularly concerned. He'd just learned he was going to be transferred to a California prison, where he knew there were a bunch of guys from his own gang and other gangs.

Rumors had been swirling since his name was mentioned in the Chandra Levy case a few years back, and some of the prisoners thought he was involved. They were saying he was a rapist. Guandique knew what happened to rapists in prisons full of gang members, who saw these men as cowards.

On the stand, Morales said, "I told him, 'Homeboy, if you ain't did nothing, you ain't got to worry.' He told me, 'Homey, you don't understand. Homeboy, I killed that bitch, but I didn't rape her.'"

Amanda Haines asked the witness to elaborate. According to the official court transcript, the testimony went as follows:

> Question: What did he tell you specifically?
> Answer: He told me he—he spotted her over there at the park.
> Q. Did he say what she was doing in the park?
> A. She was walking.

THE MAN IN THE PARK

Q. Where was he?

A. In the bushes, in the trees.

Q. And when he saw this woman, according to him, what did he tell you that he decided to do?

A. To rob her. Yeah, he was on drugs, he needed money.

Q. What did he tell you?

A. He said he hid up in the bushes. He let her get up a little ways, as soon as she passed him up a little ways, he ran up behind her, grabbed her from behind. By the neck.

Q. And then what happened, according to Mr. Guandique?

A. He dragged her into the bushes.

Q. Did he tell you what she was doing, if anything?

A. She was fighting, she was struggling. He said that by the time he got her to—to the bushes, that she had stopped struggling.

Q. And did he tell you what he made of that?

A. He thought she was unconscious or—or pretending to be unconscious.

Q. And then what did he say happened?

A. He took the pouch and left.

> Q. Now, what, if anything, did he tell you about a rape?
>
> A. He never said he raped anybody.
>
> Q. Now, what, if anything, did he tell you about whether he meant to kill her or not?
>
> A. He said he never meant to kill her. He said he never knew she was dead.

Amanda Haines then asked the witness about his state of mind. Morales explained that in the months following the alleged conversations, he'd been transferred to a different prison, where he enrolled in an educational program that had changed him; he was a new man. He'd also had a visit with his family, the first in fourteen years. On the stand, Morales claimed he wanted his family to see that he could do something good. That's why he wanted to make sure the Levys got the answers they'd been seeking for nine years.

Now it was Santha Sonenberg's turn to question Morales. She emphasized the list of crimes he had committed and tried to demonstrate that the witness was acting in his own interests, in the hope that he would be granted a reduced sentence in exchange for his testimony.

Amanda Haines repeatedly objected, while Morales maintained that he simply wanted to tell the truth.

Sonenberg kept pushing. So why was he suddenly seeking justice after a lifetime spent defying it? Had he ever cooperated with law enforcement to have his sentence reduced? Was he a snitch? And wasn't his story a bit odd? Ingmar Guandique steals a fanny pack that is never found and doesn't even realize his victim is dead?

But for Sonenberg, it was already too late. The courtroom had fallen under the spell of this forty-nine-year-old felon, his straight talk, the way he spoke of redemption.

Amanda Haines had planned to bring other witnesses to the stand, other informants, to whom Guandique had allegedly confessed his involvement during his years in prison. Some of them had been questioned by investigators in 2008 and were going to say that Guandique had boasted about raping women with other gang members, then leaving them for dead. One of them was going to describe how Guandique had raped him in prison.

In the end, none of them were asked to take the stand. Armando Morales was such a hit that the prosecution opted to go along with his story. And to do so, they would need to drop the rape charges.

On November 1, Gary Condit was called to the stand. Santha Sonenberg's strategy relied on the alternative narrative that Condit represented. The defense wanted to tell a different story: If Ingmar Guandique was such a perfect suspect, even though he didn't know Chandra, then what were they to make of this powerful man who knew her quite well and had a motive to kill?

She was looking to raise old demons from the summer of 2001. But when he took the stand, Condit didn't make much of an impression. He seemed old, deflated. He was sixty-two now and hadn't been seen on camera since his political defeat in 2002.

After spending most of 2003 driving across California alone on his motorcycle, battling depression and insomnia, Condit had spent the next few years filing defamation lawsuits against the press over articles written about him in 2001. Now, in 2010, he was keeping a low profile—or at least hoping to.

The Condit family (Gary, Carolyn, and their son Chad) had been living in Arizona since 2005, when they used the payouts from the defamation lawsuits to buy two Baskin-Robbins franchises. Ironically Chandra's favorite ice cream brand. But this new career wasn't going as Condit had hoped either. Business and politics were two very different beasts. In business, the truth is

THE MAN IN THE PARK

in the numbers, and Condit couldn't "cut a deal" with the numbers. For two years, the Condits had neglected to pay their franchise fees while continuing to sell under the Baskin-Robbins name—even though the brand had ordered that the stores be shut down, claiming the Condits owed nearly $100,000.

In 2006, Chad and Cadee were also accused of using $226,000 of funds from their father's 2001 campaign for personal gain. At the time of Chandra's murder trial, in 2010, Condit was quietly transitioning to a career in lobbying. By 2012, he would be the president of the Phoenix Institute of Desert Agriculture, and he would later go on to work as a lobbyist for a Sacramento law firm.

Although Condit was underwhelming, his mere presence was an event in itself. But his testimony turned out to be somewhat hollow. He repeated the same statements he'd been making for years. The police had mistreated him. The press had mistreated him. He felt "raped." His entire strategy seemed to rely on presenting himself as a victim of the media circus, just like Chandra.

It was a kind of rough draft for *Actual Malice: A True Crime Political Thriller*, the book he would later publish in 2015 about his experience. As *Washington Post* reporters noted, prosecutor Amanda Haines tried to make Condit look like a character from *The Bonfire of the Vanities*—a powerful, unfaithful man who'd simply been in the wrong place at the wrong time.

Next, it was the defense's turn to change the jurors' opinion of Condit. Defense attorney Maria Hawilo made no bones about it, as she approached the witness and said, flat out, "From the beginning of this case, you have lied." For many long minutes, she tried to do what so many others had attempted before her: corner Gary Condit and get him to admit to the affair. In this duel, Hawilo wielded one weapon the others had not—she reminded Condit that he was under oath. It made no difference. When she pressed him, the former congressman pulled out the same old dusty playbook, dodging her questions. Hawilo asked Judge Fisher to compel the witness to answer, but he declined.

Michael Doyle remembers that people were surprised. "The prosecution objected, and the judge ruled it was out of bounds. Which was outrageous, I thought. It would leave a supposition in the jury's mind. He should have been forced to answer. I think that was a low point of the trial."

Next, Guandique's lawyers played their last cards. First card: When the police entered Chandra's place on May 6, there were papers scattered throughout the apartment, notes that the building security had repeatedly slipped under her door to let her know her parents were looking for her. But if no one had been there since her disappearance, shouldn't they all have been in a pile near the door of her apartment?

Second card: If the killer had Chandra's keys, which were never found, he could have gone back to her apartment, perhaps on the morning of May 1, to make it look like she was online. All he'd have to do was click on her favorites for a few hours, or forward an email to her parents without adding any other comment.

The third and last card: Two unknown DNA sources were found on Chandra's leggings—one male, the other undetermined—and neither of them was a match for Ingmar Guandique, Gary Condit, or the people working in the lab analyzing the garment. The prosecutor suggested that the leggings were likely contaminated by a police officer working the scene, as had been the case with the red bra. But Guandique's lawyers were adamant—what if the mystery DNA belonged to the real killer?

❖

Throughout the trial, Susan Levy sat in the second row, in her own bubble. This was her new life. She moved through the world in a parallel dimension, next to people who had not lost their daughter.

For four weeks, she sat there almost every day, in silence. On her knees, she held a small notebook. She took notes for no reason, just for herself, and attended nearly every day of hearings, except when forensic experts were brought in to describe her daughter's remains. On those days, her spot on the bench was empty.

As it turns out, the universe sent her a sign, a brief moment of respite in the midst of all this pain. A horse show was being held in Washington, DC, and Susan, who felt soothed by the presence of her beloved horses, was able to tear away the walls of her bubble for the two-day equestrian event.

Back at the courthouse, Susan ran into Condit. They didn't speak. Why bother? The way Susan saw it, Condit had lied at the Jefferson Hotel in 2001, the one and only time they had met previously, and he had also lied on the stand nine years later.

The trial didn't give her a sense of peace. She found it discouraging and exhausting. It didn't show her anything she didn't already know. She never stopped hearing her daughter's voice, saying, "What difference does it make?" It was an expression Chandra often used. At 11:45 a.m., on Monday, November 22, the words echoed in Susan's mind as she sat in the second row and watched the nine jurors find Ingmar Guandique guilty of murdering Chandra Levy.

3.
HOUSE OF CARDS

2015:
FIVE YEARS AFTER THE TRIAL

It all started with a handful of messages on people's answering machines. Voicemails were left for Michael Doyle, other journalists, and Susan Levy. Then a Facebook message.

Susan was only half paying attention as she opened up the message from a woman claiming to have information about her daughter's murder. To Susan, it was nonsense. It wasn't the first time she'd been sent this kind of tip since Chandra's disappearance in 2001, and even since the trial in 2010. She told the stranger that any information, if she did have something, should be passed on to the US Attorney's office in DC. Then she closed the message and forgot about it.

The following year, in 2016, every newsroom in Washington, DC, was getting ready for the fifteenth anniversary of Chandra Levy's disappearance. On ABC, Michael Doyle was interviewed about the story, and as he walked back to the office after the show, he felt he'd done well. He was proud of his work.

Back in the newsroom, he was getting ready to wrap up his article about the anniversary when a press release from the prosecutor's office threw everything into question. The charges against Ingmar Guandique were being dropped. No further information was provided. Had there been a procedural error? Was there a new suspect? Would Guandique be retried? Doyle panicked. He spent the next few hours frantically making phone calls and trying to figure out what was going on, then turned in his article at the end of the day. Given the circumstances, he figured it wasn't half bad.

Back home, Doyle sat down with a beer and let out a satisfied sigh, feeling his body relax at the first sip. He was just about to put his feet up on the table when he noticed a new *Washington Post* article pop up on his screen. While his own piece had simply reported the latest updates, that the conviction had been overturned, and speculated on the reasons for the decision, his competition seemed to have all the answers. According to *The Washington Post*, an actress named Babs Proller was claiming the key witness in the Levy trial had lied.

Before Doyle could read the sentence a second time, something clicked in his head. *Babs Proller* . . . The name sounded familiar because just a few months before, he had ignored a message from Proller. Doyle explains, "By that point, I had gotten so many nutcases, I didn't return the call." But the people at *The Washington Post* did return Proller's call. And they were not disappointed.

Proller was an extra in *House of Cards*, where she'd once sat ten feet away from Kevin Spacey. It was her claim to fame, and now she had a second one. In July 2015, the fifty-one-year-old German-born actress had temporarily moved into a small hotel in Maryland. While walking her golden retriever, Buddy, around the neighborhood, she'd met a man in his fifties who called himself Phoenix, and they became friends. Phoenix would even look after Buddy when Proller was out of town.

One day, her friend confessed that he'd recently been released after serving a twenty-year jail sentence. He also told her his real name, Armando Morales, and said he'd been the star witness in the Chandra Levy murder trial. Proller was concerned but kept seeing Morales.

As she would later tell ABC in her only television interview, she decided to start recording their conversations "for her own protection." She saved seven hours of tapes, mostly recorded while Morales was helping her sort through her things at a local storage locker. Sitting on the concrete floor, with his hands deep in moving boxes, he told her all about his past as a gang member.

The way he talked made it seem like his life of crime wasn't entirely behind him. For instance, when Proller was having problems with a man who'd allegedly stolen some of her jewelry, Morales offered to "take care of it." This was not the Morales who'd testified five years earlier and spoken of redemption. For a few minutes, he also described Guandique's confessions.

Eventually, Proller sent the recordings to the prosecutor's office because of the Guandique statements and tried to notify the press. In the ABC interview, she claimed Morales admitted to lying on the stand because the prosecutor wanted him to. He said they were sure they had the right guy but needed someone to say it. And yet, this conversation is nowhere to be found in the recordings. The press and the prosecutor's office never did get to hear it.

Proller wouldn't make a great witness either. In 2012, she was charged with theft in Pennsylvania, and she changed her name several times (following two marriages and two divorces, says Proller). Everyone who came into direct contact with her—like Michael Doyle, when he eventually called her back, and Susan Levy—remembers her as a very strange woman. But the law can't work with "strange" claims, it relies only on facts.

And in 2016, it was faced with a few unequivocal facts. Armando Morales was no longer a reliable witness. He'd lied about redemption, and his side of the story was not as convincing as it had been on the stand. Ingmar Guandique's lawyers also discovered that, contrary to what Morales had implied at the trial, this was not his first time acting as an informant for law enforcement. In the past, he'd also contacted them to provide intel about crimes committed by his own gang.

The judge ordered a retrial. But on July 28, 2016, the second trial, which had been scheduled to begin the following fall, was canceled. This time, the judge dismissed the case entirely, citing insufficient evidence. On May 8, 2017, Ingmar Guandique was deported to El Salvador, a free man. He vanished.

JUSTICE FOR CHANDRA

1.
THE COVER-UP

He suggested we meet at Tryst, the Adams Morgan coffee shop just a four-minute walk from Condit's former apartment. This is where the congressman and Chandra spent one of their rare moments together in public. Today, more than twenty years later, the high Art Deco ceiling is the same, but more modern versions of Chandra sit around the tables, wearing AirPods and working while they sip lavender lemonade.

In this crowd, Ralph Daugherty sticks out like a sore thumb. He's seventy-one years old now, and his body isn't what it used to be. His legs can't take him scrambling through Rock Creek Park anymore, and he's a little hard of hearing. But his memory is all there. Although he's an IT guy and never lived in DC, he knows the area like the back of his hand—the Adams Morgan and Dupont Circle neighborhoods, Rock Creek Park . . . all the locations that were relevant in the Chandra Levy investigation.

In 2001, when the case blew up, Daugherty was forty-nine and living in Columbus, Ohio. He had been divorced for years, had no children, and was working at the Bath & Body Works headquarters.

Daugherty had never been all that interested in the news and crime stories. He didn't even watch TV. But he remembers how, at the time, the Chandra Drama had become this kind of background noise in every part of America. It was only in July 2001 that the case finally caught his attention, when the police released Chandra's search history, listing the thirty-six sites she'd browsed over three hours.

As an IT guy, Daugherty took a look at the URLs, curious to see if a clue might stand out. It's hard to explain why he was so keen. The story just drew him to it, as though he had leaned too close and fallen into the case. He searched the web for any discussion boards or forums and found a site called chandra-levy.com, where hundreds of users were having conversations, sharing their theories, and looking for clues.

Ralph joined in and logged on every day. Initially, he wondered why no one was pushing Condit a little

JUSTICE FOR CHANDRA

harder. Shortly after Chandra's body was found in the park, the chandra-levy.com website was shut down. This was no longer a missing persons case, and the forum administrators, who had probably hoped to make some money, figured it was over.

But Daugherty wasn't ready for everything to stop, so he started his own forum, where he stored everything that had already been posted and compiled. He called it justiceforchandra.com. Almost three hundred people followed him over to this new website, and about fifty of them posted regularly. When Daugherty launched his website, Reddit wasn't the powerhouse it is today, and social networks didn't exist at all. So, the forum became this gathering place for anyone who was still wondering what had happened to Chandra Levy.

As of today, the site has an archive of 26,244 posts, featuring news articles, theories, results from research done on the ground, ideas, and comments. And the leads just keep coming. Isn't it strange that the gym employee who was the last person to see Chandra alive goes by several names? Could Minister Otis Thomas have lied? Could Gary Condit be the father of Otis Thomas's grandchild?

Some of the usernames come up often, but even Daugherty doesn't know who's behind each one. He's never met them in real life, doesn't know much about them, and wants to give them privacy. He does, however, share that many users are women who are quite upset with the way the media treats women in general and how they are abused by men. Other posters are true crime buffs. As for Daugherty, he's fascinated by the DC police's attitude toward Condit. In his mind, the crime was never truly investigated and the authorities left many stones unturned.

In 2003, Daugherty made his first trip to DC. He had just been fired from Bath & Body Works and had a few free months ahead of him, so he figured it was now or never. This was his opportunity to hit the road and write the book he'd been thinking about for two years. He retraced Chandra's footsteps throughout the city, with his watch in hand. On September 17, 2003, he posted this message on the forum, with a few photos: "I am sitting at the picnic table at #18. Where Chandra was found is behind me and over the hill. The reporting has just been pathetic when you take a look at what she was supposed to have done to get here to be attacked, how isolated this spot is [. . .]. More details when I have a chance. I'm going back down over the hill again to Broad Branch. I want to see what a turtle hunter and his dog would see from down there."

JUSTICE FOR CHANDRA

Today, he recalls walking along a dirt trail for a while, trying to imagine Chandra strolling through the park, lost in thought, listening to music. That day, his daydreaming was cut short when the path became a little harder to follow. Then he got lost. There were no signs nearby. He hoisted his laptop bag up higher on his shoulder, then made his way up and down trails that all seemed to peter out. Somehow, disoriented, he emerged from the woods and ended up on a sidewalk. As he left the park, out of breath, Daugherty felt even more certain about his theory: Chandra would never have come out here for a stroll.

Daugherty took his investigation all the way to Luray, Virginia. That's where Condit made a call to Anne Marie Smith, his flight attendant mistress, at midnight on May 17, 2001. The media circus surrounding his relationship with Chandra had intensified, and Smith was demanding an explanation.

But why call from Luray? What was he doing there? There was nothing in Luray, really, just a few streets, a McDonald's, and a gas station. The fast food joint closed at 11:00 p.m., and the gas station shut down at 9:00 p.m. So Condit had waited for everything to be closed, for the intersection to be quiet and pitch black, before using the pay phone. What was he doing there so late? Condit never explained himself.

Daugherty stood in the same phone booth, at the same time, looking around, trying to understand. On the way there, he couldn't help but notice the names of the roadside hotels, restaurants, and other attractions. Grand Caverns, Skyline Caverns, Endless Caverns, Shenandoah Caverns. Luray was at the heart of cave country, and many of the caves and caverns were tourist attractions. They were everywhere—big and small, dug into rock, isolated. Was Condit trying to get rid of something?

That same evening, on May 17, Bob and Susan Levy had been interviewed on *The Larry King Show*. Maybe Condit had just been trying to get away from the media frenzy that was consuming his life? Whatever the reason, he likely drove to Luray, probably in that red Ford Fiesta he'd forgotten to mention to the police. In fact, investigators had no clue Condit even owned this car until Smith told them he'd sometimes used it to pick her up. One of his aides, Mike Dayton, kept it at his place and was the one driving it most of the time. By the time the vehicle was searched and analyzed, several weeks had gone by.

After conducting his own investigation of key locations in Chandra Levy's disappearance, Daugherty went back home and, in 2004, wrote a three-hundred-page book called *Murder on a Horse Trail: The Disappearance of Chandra Levy*. It features the results of his research, a compilation of news articles, and comments from regular posters on the forum. On May 1, 2004, Daugherty released the self-published book to mark the three-year anniversary of Chandra's death. He dedicated it to the Levys.

The word "cover-up" comes up again and again on justiceforchandra.com. Posters are skeptical about a lot of things in this case, such as the way Chandra's internship had come to an abrupt end. Several of them scoured the USC website to learn about its internship policies. One well-informed user mentioned that the form submitted to terminate Chandra's internship typically had a "two- to four-week" processing time, so why was she fired on the spot? "What happened to her is not normal procedure. She was just told one day to leave, 'See ya!' The timing of it," he says, referring to the fact that just one week before her disappearance, she'd confronted Condit about what Otis Thomas had told her mom.

Her application for a job at the FBI was found, but only the hard copy and not the digital one, which could have slowed down the processing time for her application. Daugherty has wondered whether someone was trying to make Chandra leave town. And, like any

IT guy, Daugherty is also curious about the computer crash at Chandra's apartment—a cop hits a few keys on her laptop and suddenly it's compromised to such an extent that it has to be sent to a private lab, which will then take two months to recover her data? "We didn't know that at the time. It was revealed at the trial. How did they destroy the hardware? If we'd known then, it would have made a lot of noise," he says emphatically. Daugherty is right. In 2010, during Guandique's trial, an expert witness was unable to explain what happened to the hard drive.

But Daugherty and his crew are most concerned by yet another piece of information that has long remained under the radar. On April 30, 2001, the day before Chandra disappeared, a scream was heard inside the Newport. It was 4:37 a.m. A neighbor called the cops, and a patrol was sent out. The police found nothing unusual. From the beginning, law enforcement assumed that since Chandra was active on her computer the following morning, the scream had nothing to do with her. Daugherty and his online crew are well aware that if Chandra had been killed or kidnapped overnight, in her home, her attackers would have had to leave the building with her body and get by the doorman. Still, they can't stop thinking about the scream. They keep hearing it.

Cover-up, cover-up, cover-up.

Over a coffee, Daugherty admits that in the forum, no one seems to believe the Guandique angle. "Guandique? No, I never thought it was him . . . The only thing for Guandique is that, yes, he did attack women in the park in July, and that's it." Daugherty explains that the attacks may have been close to where Chandra's body was found, but there was still a steep hill in between the locations. We know he attacked them with a knife—Halle Shilling and Christy Wiegand both described this in court. But Chandra wasn't stabbed. The autopsy report states there were no stab wounds on her bones, and there were no bloodstains on the clothes found in the park.

So if we are to believe the story told by Armando Morales, Guandique would have accidentally killed her, as he dragged her by the neck, before they even left the footpath and went into the woods?

Daugherty thinks the robbery theory, used in the 2010 conviction, doesn't hold water either. On May 7, a week after he allegedly killed Chandra in the park, Guandique was arrested when he was caught burglarizing an apartment from which he stole a gold wedding ring. In his mugshot, Guandique should still have some injuries from the altercation with Chandra—the scratches on his face and the swollen lip that witnesses described at the trial. Except the mugshot was never made public.

And if Guandique had been robbing people for financial gain—like when he stole that gold ring during the home burglary—then where was Chandra's jewelry? The police search never turned up the bracelet Condit had given Chandra, the keys to her apartment, and a small, custom, fourteen-karat gold ring her parents had bought for her in Modesto. It was a graduation gift, and her initials were engraved on the inside.

Investigators checked all the pawnshops in the area. But none of them carried Chandra's jewelry. If Guandique had her jewelry, wouldn't he have tried to pawn it? Now, you could suggest that if Guandique had accidentally killed Chandra, he might have been scared and opted to get rid of the jewelry in another way. But this theory doesn't line up with the story told by Morales, who claimed Guandique was unaware that Chandra had died. And if Guandique did know he'd killed her, it seems highly unlikely he'd go back to the same area just a few days after the murder to prey on a new victim.

Daugherty points out another disturbing fact: The keys should have been found in or around the park, even long after the crime. If the killer didn't know Chandra,

JUSTICE FOR CHANDRA

they would have had no use for her keys. Only someone close to her would have known her address and elected to keep the keys.

❖

The people who post on Daugherty's forum may be anonymous, amateur sleuths, but they aren't the only ones rejecting the Ingmar Guandique theory. Chandra's aunt, Linda Zamsky, never believed he was guilty. When he was arrested in 2009, she didn't feel relief. She, too, couldn't help but wonder about a cover-up.

For the past twenty-three years, she's been certain that Condit was involved. To explain, she holds up three fingers. One, Chandra wouldn't have gone anywhere without her phone. She always took it with her, even when she was just going for a walk around Zamsky's home in Maryland. Two, Condit lied, and he never stopped lying, throughout this case. Three, the police demonstrated extreme negligence.

Zamsky does not have fond memories of the investigators. When she first went to DC with her husband to tell them what she knew, she was given a cold welcome, then sent to an interrogation room as if she were a criminal. Zamsky told the investigators everything she knew about Condit, how he had a lot of cacti in his apartment, the color of the walls, his favorite ice cream, all the secrets Chandra had shared. But it felt like they didn't trust her.

Today, with her eyes wide open, she wonders aloud—what reason would she have had to lie about a man she had never met?

In the spring of 2001, a few weeks after the interrogation that left a bitter taste in Zamsky's mouth, the FBI came to her home in Maryland. At this point, Zamsky had already spoken to *The Washington Post*. The two agents believed her story. They asked her to repeat what she'd already told DC police and, above all, told her to be very careful. "Keep your eyes open, be aware of your surroundings."

Detective Joe McCann never believed Guandique was guilty either. This usual suspect was too convenient. His blue eyes are steady when he says, "You could build a case on anybody." The way he sees it, the case against Guandique was weak, very weak. "Why are we gonna move on Guandique when we don't have a case against him? We've got a jailhouse snitch and some scratches on him. Why?" he asks rhetorically. "'Cause we want it to go away. I brought murder cases to prosecutors, who told me 'We can't prosecute that, come back with more evidence.'"

McCann figures Guandique was charged, despite a lack of evidence, to make the case go away. Or maybe to ensure someone else wouldn't eventually be charged. McCann doesn't mince words. He describes how law enforcement and the courts were pressured to swiftly deliver a conviction on a suspect that suited everyone. He's given it a lot of thought. McCann spent two years on the Chandra Levy case, then so many more mulling over questions. But he still has no answers. He keeps asking, "Why, why, why?" as he looks off into the distance.

Over time, people living with doubt get worn down; they need to build theories and weave together shreds of imagination so they can learn to live with the uncertainty. McCann can't let go of the idea that not all evidence was brought to light. This is not what he spent two years looking for. Ingmar Guandique is not his answer. He figures there's another rapist, someone nobody has discovered. Or maybe a "friend" of Condit's played a role in her death.

Linda Zamsky also sits alone with her doubts. She thinks Chandra might have asked Condit for more, handed him an ultimatum as her patience began to wear thin. Was she killed because she was a threat to his career, this congressman who was a potential candidate for the Democratic primaries in 2004?

Joe McCann and Linda Zamsky think Chandra may have gone to the park to meet someone, and then what happened? An ultimatum gone wrong? Condit could, for example, have sent one of his loyal assistants to take care of the breakup for him. With the red car, maybe? Or maybe he showed up himself, then was taken aback by his mistress's determination. A lot of things could have happened. Over the past twenty-three years, theories have proliferated. They bubble up to the surface, and some take a while to burst.

2.
THE HORSE WHISPERER

There is a conspiracy theory out there about the term "conspiracy theory." Apparently, the words "conspiracy" and "theory" were first used together in 1967, by the CIA, in an attempt to discredit people who doubted the official account of JFK's assassination by Lee Harvey Oswald, painting them as fringe kooks. In reality, the term was already used in books dating back to the nineteenth century and became mainstream in the 1950s. One thing's for sure—conspiracy theorists went into overdrive after 9/11, and they were unlikely to steer clear of the Chandra Levy case.

In May 2002, when the young intern's bones were found in Rock Creek Park, a new theory began to take shape. What if the CIA—*it's always the CIA*—had been aware of imminent terrorist attacks months before September 11, so they'd dumped Chandra's remains in the park and made sure they would be found quickly, thus drawing public attention away from 9/11 suspicions? The idea never fully died out, and, to this day, it's all over YouTube and obscure online forums.

And it's certainly not the only conspiracy theory surrounding the Chandra Levy case. Almost every one hinges on the same fact: Condit was a member of the House Intelligence Committee and therefore had access to top-secret information. What did he share with his young mistress, intentionally or maybe inadvertently? Perhaps he'd mentioned 9/11. Was Chandra taken out because she knew what was going to happen that fateful morning?

Surprisingly, Condit put forward his own conspiracy theory in his book, *Actual Malice*. He recalls one time they met at Tryst. "At 8:00 p.m., Chandra's unmistakable mass of curls bounced as she entered Tryst," he begins. According to Condit, she told him something she'd heard at the office: Timothy McVeigh, who was on death row for the 1995 Oklahoma City bombing, was scheduled to be executed in two months, but his lawyers were claiming the government had failed to provide all required documents to the defense at his trial. They were suggesting the FBI was aware of other people who had potentially been involved in the attack.

At the time, Chandra was working at the Federal Bureau of Prisons. Visibly thrilled to be in on the secret, she told him the execution would have to be postponed.

Condit was surprised that such sensitive information would be shared with an intern. Some people have interpreted this as Condit saying his government, the government he worked for, might have wanted to get rid of a young woman who knew too much. But even if this assumption is right, Chandra wouldn't have been killed for that specific bit of information because it was made public in May 2001, shortly after her disappearance. Moreover, even after McVeigh's lawyers finally were granted access to the missing documents, he was executed on June 11, 2001.

❖

The theory cooked up by Dominick Dunne may be the one to have traveled the farthest. A former Hollywood producer turned novelist in the eighties, Dunne was the brother of writer John Gregory Dunne. In 1982, Dominick Dunne's daughter was murdered by her ex-boyfriend, and Dunne covered the ensuing trial for *Vanity Fair*, then wrote a book about it.

Over the years, he gradually became a crime reporter, working on the trials of O. J. Simpson and Phil Spector. Unsurprisingly, Dunne, who had written *An Inconvenient Woman* a decade before, was fascinated by the Chandra Levy case from the moment it hit the newsstands. In this story, he wanted to glimpse the pinnacle of every obsession he'd depicted in his novels: the secrets of the rich and powerful and how they always managed to get away with it.

In the fall of 2001, Dunne, now seventy-six, started to tell a wild tale at the social lunches that were the fabric of his life. *He* knew what had happened to Chandra Levy. He told it to some of his journalist friends in November 2001. He told it to Laura Ingraham, a journalist who had just launched her radio show in December. Then he told his story to *Vanity Fair*, and then on TV. Dominick Dunne was willing to tell his story to anyone who would listen, and did so until the day Chandra's body was found.

Dunne's tale begins in October 2001, when he first received a call from Hamburg, Germany. The caller was a man who had information about the missing intern. Apparently, Dunne had said, on some TV program, that

Chandra might have been riding a motorcycle and that the Hells Angels were definitely involved in the whole thing. But the man on the line wanted Dunne to know he was dead wrong—he knew the real story. He made Dunne promise to keep his identity secret, and thus the source became known as the "Horse Whisperer," since he claimed the famous novel (and subsequent film adaptation) were based on his story.

According to Dunne, his source was a horse dealer who worked with clients in the US, Europe, and the Middle East, especially catering to the wealthy Emirati sheikhs. On one of his work trips, the Horse Whisperer had met an individual who was tasked with procuring very young women for the sheikhs and their friends during their travels. Dunne hung on to his every word, frantically scribbling it all down.

On the other end of the line, the source went on. This pimp had told him Condit was one of his bosses' powerful friends and that he and his aide Mike Dayton often attended underground parties at Middle East embassies in DC. But what did this all have to do with Chandra? It was quite simple. Apparently, Condit had complained to his Middle Eastern friends about this "clingy" mistress and how he'd made her promises he couldn't keep, and now she wouldn't accept it was over. But the bigger issue was that she knew things about him that could be damning if she went public. He didn't know what to do.

So Condit's friends allegedly decided to take matters into their own hands, although Dunne was unclear on whether this happened with or without the congressman's consent. The pimp witnessed Chandra's kidnapping. Five men put her in a black limousine—she seemed to have been drugged and wasn't struggling. Then they loaded her into a plane and dumped her over the Atlantic Ocean.

Until May 2002, the story was a crowd favorite at high-society parties. It made its way throughout New York and DC, and Dunne was asked to tell it over and over again. No one had to twist his arm. Sometimes the end of the story was tweaked, just a little, with Chandra becoming a sex slave in the Middle East. But that wasn't Dunne's work—the rumor had come alive, grown independent of its creator, traveling, mutating. In May 2002, when Chandra's body was found, the rumor died off, and everyone forgot about it.

Everyone, that is, except Gary Condit. In January 2005, the former congressman filed a defamation lawsuit against Dunne for $11 million. The Horse Whisperer's identity would be shared in court. His name was Monty Roberts, and he was a famous horse trainer, but he was not one of the three people who inspired the author of *The Horse Whisperer*. And although he was well liked in the equestrian world, Roberts had been accused of animal abuse and fraud. According to his family, his autobiography was nothing more than a pack of lies.

In the end, Condit agreed to settle out of court, but the amount paid out was never disclosed. Dominick Dunne died of cancer four years later, in 2009.

3.
SERIAL KILLER

Christine Mirzayan.
Joyce Chiang.
Chandra Levy.

Twentysomethings, petite, dark-haired, pretty. Murdered in 1998, 1999, and 2001.

What if Chandra's disappearance had nothing to do with Condit or Guandique? What if it was the work of a serial killer operating in the Washington area?

In the summer of 1998, twenty-eight-year-old Christine Mirzayan was finishing her PhD in biochemistry and working as an intern at the National Academy of Sciences, which advises the US government on issues related to science. She was born in Tehran to Armenian parents and had moved to California when she was nine.

After studying at Yale and UC San Francisco, she'd ended up in Washington, DC, where she had a job lined up for the fall and an apartment in Georgetown. Her husband would soon be joining her in DC.

On August 1, she called him up just before heading out to meet friends for a barbecue. On her way home from dinner, she was walking down Canal Road, which runs along the Potomac River, when someone pushed her into the woods, sexually assaulted her, then killed her with a seventy-three-pound rock. Her body was found the next morning. A bystander had actually heard her screams but didn't spot anything unusual when he stepped closer to the woods. Another witness had seen a man run off a little later and was able to describe his build. Despite all this evidence, and despite the fact that DNA was collected, the murder was yet to be solved.

Less than six months later, on January 9, 1999, a Taiwanese American woman named Joyce Chiang, aged twenty-eight, was on her way home in the Dupont Circle neighborhood. She'd just had dinner with friends at Lauriol Plaza, a Mexican restaurant on 18th Street NW. It was early, not yet 8:30 p.m., but Chiang was tired after a long week at work, where she was a lawyer with the US Immigration and Naturalization Service. She'd also been fighting off a cold since New Year's Eve.

Her friends offered to drive her home, and although she didn't want to inconvenience them, she accepted the lift because it was cold out. Chiang didn't have a car—she hated driving. It had even become a joke among her friends—someone always ended up giving her a ride home, and it was an opportunity to chat.

That night, Chiang asked to be dropped off at the Starbucks on the corner of Connecticut Avenue and R Street NW. As she stepped out of the car, she thanked her friend and pulled her hood up over her head, tightening it to keep the cold breeze out. She ordered an herbal green tea and left Starbucks. Her apartment was a ten-minute walk away. She vanished.

❖

When, a year and a half later, Chandra Levy moved to Dupont Circle, the missing person flyers with Chiang's photo were all gone or had been washed out by the rain.

Chandra went to that same Starbucks. And the Newport was less than a mile from Chiang's old apartment. The day after Chiang went missing, a couple found her wallet in Anacostia Park. Since the young woman had been a federal employee, the FBI led the investigation. Officers found her keys, gloves, and torn jacket in the

JUSTICE FOR CHANDRA

same area, but then the investigation stalled. Finally, on April 1, three months after that winter night, a man was out canoeing on the Potomac when he spotted a decomposing body. It had washed up eight miles from where Chiang's belongings were found.

DNA analyses later confirmed the remains were those of Joyce Chiang, but no further conclusions could be made from the autopsy, as the body had been in the water for months. As would later be the case with Chandra Levy, there were no obvious injuries, so it was impossible to establish the cause of death, whether Chiang had drowned or died before ending up in the water, and whether she'd been sexually assaulted. The police were calling it a homicide but weren't ruling out an accident or suicide.

Over time, the case was forgotten. There were other missing women, more murders. Joyce Chiang's name wasn't mentioned again until Chandra disappeared in May 2001. The two young women had a lot in common, and they were government employees. People began to wonder if they'd both been killed by the same person.

Condit was one of the first to give credence to this rumor. In a letter sent to his constituents in the summer of 2001, he implied as much, stating, "I pray that she has not met the same fate as the other young women who have disappeared from the same neighborhood."

The letter irked Assistant Chief of Police Terrance Gainer, who had already run out of patience for Condit. At the end of the summer, Gainer told the press that although the Joyce Chiang case had not been resolved, he and his colleagues now deemed it a suicide.

Just as they would later do with Chandra—who was portrayed as desperate over a breakup and the loss of her internship—the police served up Chiang's past to the public. They dredged up old stories about a colleague with whom she'd had a romantic relationship, one that had ended a few months before her death.

The Immigration and Naturalization Service had allegedly launched an internal investigation in response to a complaint filed by this colleague, who claimed Chiang had spread false rumors about him. Chiang was scheduled to be interrogated at the time of her disappearance. Meanwhile, despite the fact that her brother Roger insisted the couple had broken up long before her death and that Chiang had moved on, the police continued to view a suicide as the most likely explanation. There was no way they were going to mention the words "serial killer."

The Metro PD could believe whatever it wanted to, but an actual serial killer was, in fact, roaming the city at the time. Today, he's known as the Potomac River Rapist, charged with ten counts of sexual assault and one murder.

When DNA results finally came in, it was found he had killed Christine Mirzayan on August 1, 1998. Had he lost control, or was it an act of violence in a pattern of escalation? We'll never know. Mirzayan was his last known victim, but it would still take years for the killer to be identified and apprehended.

In 2011, the FBI launched a web page, published articles, and started a podcast to gather clues that might bring this cold case back to life. They also began working with Parabon NanoLabs, a company that helps identify criminals using DNA from other family members, collected from multiple genealogy sites.

Parabon gave the police the names of five men who they believed might be the Potomac River Rapist, and on November 13, 2019, the FBI arrested sixty-year-old Giles Warrick in South Carolina. He pleaded not guilty in 2021. Almost three years to the day after his arrest, and as his trial was about to begin in November 2022, Warrick was found dead in his cell. He had killed himself.

Joyce Chiang's case also has a bitter ending. In January 2011, twelve years after the young woman's death, the police announced that they had solved the murder and would be closing the case. No further details were provided.

Eventually, a journalist who was close to the victim's brother found out that investigators had identified two men suspected of kidnapping Joyce to rob her. The police claimed the suspects had driven her to the Potomac and dumped her in the river, or that Chiang had slipped while trying to get away.

One of the suspects was already serving a life sentence in Maryland for another crime, and the other was living in Guyana, South America, where the US had no powers of extradition.

❖

Why didn't the Joyce Chiang case stir up a media frenzy like the Chandra Drama? Susan Levy is well aware that her daughter's disappearance would not have been so high profile if it hadn't been for her relationship with a US congressman.

But there was probably something else at play. Americans call this the Missing White Woman Syndrome. According to stats from the National Missing and Unidentified Persons System, roughly six hundred

JUSTICE FOR CHANDRA

thousand people go missing in the United States every year. And although Black people make up just under one-sixth of the US population, they account for one-third of missing persons. Conversely, three-quarters of Americans are white, but they make up only half of the missing persons list.

Few people have studied the way in which the media covers missing persons cases and crimes, but in 2013, a researcher at Northwestern University named Zach Sommers analyzed articles published by four American media outlets, including CNN, over the course of a single year. He found that half of the articles on missing persons were about white women, and that media coverage for these cases was much more intense and longer-lasting than it was for nonwhite women and for men.

Case in point, the juxtaposition of Chandra Levy's and Joyce Chiang's disappearances. While Chiang was quickly forgotten, it would take the disappearance of Chandra Levy, a young white woman from a well-to-do family, to bring Chiang back in the press. "There's something about the missing, young, beautiful white woman that has a lot of symbolic weight in America. It's an aberration, and it becomes a container for things like the loss of innocence or the death of purity," explained researcher and author Jean Murley in an interview with *The New Yorker*.

Despite her sensational affair with a congressman, when Chandra disappeared, she became America's "girl next door," the college friend, the neighbor, the young colleague . . . She was described—especially before the affair came out—as a funny, passionate young woman who couldn't stand injustice and had a promising future. She was described as serious, careful, and well raised. She was getting her master's degree and had career plans. These are the classic traits of the Missing White Woman. She is seen as someone's sister, daughter, mother.

On the other hand, when a nonwhite woman disappears in the United States, the focus tends to be on the dysfunctional aspects of her life, those that may have led to her demise. The coverage is rarely about her successes. Over the years, this phenomenon has been further analyzed and other criteria have emerged, including the victim's class and age. The closer the victim gets to the cliché of a "damsel in distress"—white, young, middle-class or upper-class—the more her disappearance will be covered by the media. In 2001, the year Chandra disappeared, 231 murders and 181 rapes were committed in DC alone. But no case got more attention than hers.

Susan Levy has had time to reflect on it. She often says, "At the time, we didn't think about that." The Levys weren't thinking about the way in which the press would portray their daughter, they weren't thinking about the way people would talk about them, they weren't thinking about the way the photo they chose would be perceived, and they weren't thinking about overexposure and the media backlash it might cause. In 2001, and in the first few months of 2002, Chandra's parents were obsessed with only one thing: finding their daughter, at all costs.

Susan didn't even notice that the press found her too noisy, too present. Bob didn't notice people were saying he'd lost his mind. Linda Zamsky didn't notice that Washington journalists had, at one point, claimed she had a drug addiction. And they didn't anticipate how Chandra's disappearance would affect their acquaintances and friends. They explain how Chandra's godmother, Fran, "tried to be a detective." "She got too involved," Bob grumbles, while Susan can only sigh and say, "People do what they can . . ."

Susan lost a lot of girlfriends. As soon as Chandra disappeared, Susan joined a support group for relatives of missing persons. At first, it did provide support. But as the Chandra case increasingly took up oxygen in the media, pushing everything else to the margins, obliterating any other news, resentment thickened around her. The group eventually split up.

"At the time, we weren't thinking about that," she says again. Nothing else seemed to exist but this desperate hope that they could find Chandra, her curly-haired girl with a high-pitched voice and dry wit. And when that hope collapsed, the Levys' lives went up in smoke.

EPILOGUE

Carl Moultrie Courthouse, February 11, 2011. Susan Levy was on autopilot. She stood up, not knowing how her legs were still carrying her weight. Her body had been full of surprises over the past ten years. She hadn't known you could survive an entire decade after the death of your child.

She took the stand, a few sheets of paper in hand. She didn't know if she should look at him or not. She didn't know anymore whether it would do her good or break her heart. But, then again, what was left of her heart anyway? It was decimated, just like everything else in her world.

Two and a half months before, Ingmar Guandique had been found guilty of murdering Chandra. It had been nine years, nine months, and ten days since her death. And on this day, Susan and Bob were back. They'd taken that damned flight again, five hours and eleven minutes probably spent thinking of nothing but her, always her, to get to this damned capital that had swallowed up their daughter. Guandique would soon be sentenced to sixty years in prison.

Bob didn't want to speak. The truth was he hadn't been saying much for about ten years. Susan was going to say a few words. She read a poem, softly. At first, her voice was so quiet it was hard to hear. As she read, her anger swelled, working its way up her throat, gaining momentum. Susan was speaking for Bob too. She spoke about her husband's parents and how they'd survived the Holocaust. How all this—all the misfortune, the violence, the brutal collision with tragedy—had brought their pain back to the surface. She said that the past ten years had been a living nightmare from which she could never wake up.

Then Susan turned to Ingmar Guandique. "How can you take my daughter's life away?" she said. "Did you really take her? Look me in my eyes and tell me." Guandique shook his head as if to say "No." She called him a "hideous creature," "lower than a cockroach."

Judge Fisher interrupted, instructing Susan to address only him, as she could not speak directly to the

EPILOGUE

defendant. Susan was quiet. No one was going to tell her who she could and couldn't talk to.

All those cops, those lawyers, this so-called justice system . . . What had they done for her, and for her daughter? Her anger was back. Susan took one last look at the judge, then turned back to Guandique and spat, "And finally, *fuck you*!" and returned to her spot on the bench.

❖

It's September 2023, and Bob and Susan have changed. They are now over seventy years old. The anger is gone. It left behind something else, the will to live as Chandra would have wanted and the refusal to become "bad people."

Chandra dreamed of going to Antarctica, so they did. Every year, they travel. Today, they are passing through Paris on their way to Italy. Three weeks in the south, starting with Naples. After each trip, they always return to the house on Chenault Drive, which they never left.

Over time, people stopped mentioning Chandra around them. But the tragedy is lodged in all parts of the home, like bullet holes in the walls. Adam, Chandra's little brother, spent years in therapy, and Bob won't go back to Linda's house in Chesapeake City because that's where he last saw Chandra. As a family, they don't talk about it anymore. "We seem functional, but sometimes we're not," Susan whispers. They look for photos on their phones. "How does this thing work again?"

Chandra's parents cut each other off, as couples do when they've been married for ages. They know it's a miracle that they're still together. Bob lights up when he talks about his daughter, and sometimes he cries. You can see the pain rise from his gut to his eyes, squeezing his throat and forcing him to take a deep breath. He gets upset when he can't remember, as if misplacing pieces of her was unbearable.

Here are the photos. There's one of Chandra in Tanzania, sticking her tongue out after drinking something black, a giraffe in the background. There are several photos from one of Susan's art exhibitions in 2017. They show paintings, drawings, and a montage made up of photos of Chandra, baseball cards, and ladybugs.

One piece of work was never exhibited: It's a collage Susan made of Gary Condit, years ago. The congressman's face is in the center, and all around him, missiles explode as they crash into his head, while in one corner, a small figure in an orange prison jumpsuit is decapitated, with Condit's face glued onto the rolling head. Blood splashes across the canvas and sprays onto a small

EPILOGUE

photo of Chandra at the edge of it all. Susan keeps that one in a closet.

❖

On February 11, 2011, the words Susan directed at Guandique were those of a mother addressing her daughter's murderer. Today, the Levys don't believe he did it anymore. "I thought he was [guilty] at the time," Bob whispers. Susan adds, "They never proved it, I feel. I acted as if. 'Cause I needed to."

In their eyes, the evidence against Ingmar Guandique was never that strong. And time hasn't healed all wounds. First, there's the lack of closure. And there was no shortage of disappointments: the overturned conviction in 2016, Guandique's release in 2017, then yet another twist, in 2023. On July 31, 2023, the DC Court of Appeals Board on Professional Responsibility determined that prosecutor Amanda Haines had not provided the defense with the full memo on witness Armando Morales. On the missing page was information about how the witness had a history of working with law enforcement, information that Guandique's lawyers deemed crucial. Susan and Bob just shrug. Over time, Susan has come to realize that "justice" really meant "just us."

Twenty-three years later, she still thinks Condit's hands are not clean. She wonders if Chandra may have known the congressman before moving to Washington. Chandra could have crossed paths with Condit in 2000, during her four-month internship at Governor Gray Davis's Sacramento office, as the two men were quite close. She might have met Condit's kids, too, as both also worked for Davis, although Cadee and Chad Condit have always maintained that they never met her. And Chandra never talked about them.

Still, the idea settled into people's minds. Condit's driver said that, early in the summer of 2000, his boss told him about a new mistress who sounded just like Chandra. Susan wonders if perhaps Chandra landed that coveted DC internship thanks to Condit. Maybe she'd even chosen the Newport apartment to be close to him? But then . . . Susan stops herself. What would it change anyway?

Bob is more interested in another theory. He's come back to it several times and recommends reading a book by ufologist Dr. Steven Greer. In 1993, he created the Disclosure Project to prove that the American government knows about the existence of extraterrestrials and their activities, and to protect whistleblowers.

EPILOGUE 191

Bob explains that, on May 9, 2001, Dr. Greer organized a major press conference in Washington, DC, bringing together twenty people willing to testify before Congress to share what they had seen and how the government had tried to silence them. The revelations, which Dr. Greer describes as "the greatest secret of the twentieth century," were going to shake up the whole country. But Chandra's disappearance had just begun to make headlines, and journalists granted the press conference little to no coverage.

Today, Bob wonders if perhaps Condit told Chandra a little too much about UFOs, Greer's conference, and the government's role in all of it. As a member of the Intelligence Committee, who knows what secrets he was privy to.

Susan also recalls a phone call from Chandra shortly after she realized who her daughter was dating. "He believes in those UFO stories like you, Mom," Chandra had confided. Bob's been thinking about it a lot these days because in July 2023, the US Congress finally held a hearing on what are now known as UAPs (unidentified aerial phenomena). That day, former US Air Force Major David Grusch claimed the US government had been monitoring "nonhuman" activity since the 1930s. When asked by a lawmaker whether anyone might have been murdered to cover up information, Grusch replied that he was unable to answer the question publicly. Bob couldn't help but think of Chandra.

❖

In Paris, Susan wears a bracelet with ladybugs on it. "Ladybug" had been Chandra's nickname since summer camp. Over the past twenty-three years, every time Susan and Bob have seen a ladybug, it has felt like a sign, a visit from their daughter. It happened in Berlin, Moscow, Finland, Mongolia . . . For a moment, they smiled. Susan gently touches the bracelet.

She goes through the photos, starts to tell a story. When Chandra was born, in the hospital, the nurses accidentally gave Susan the wrong baby. She was handed a newborn and began breastfeeding without paying much attention. Turns out the baby was a boy. When she realized the mistake, Susan laughed and finished feeding him anyway. Where was her daughter in that moment? She doesn't know. She's not sure why she's sharing this story. Maybe she was always meant to lose Chandra.

APPENDICES

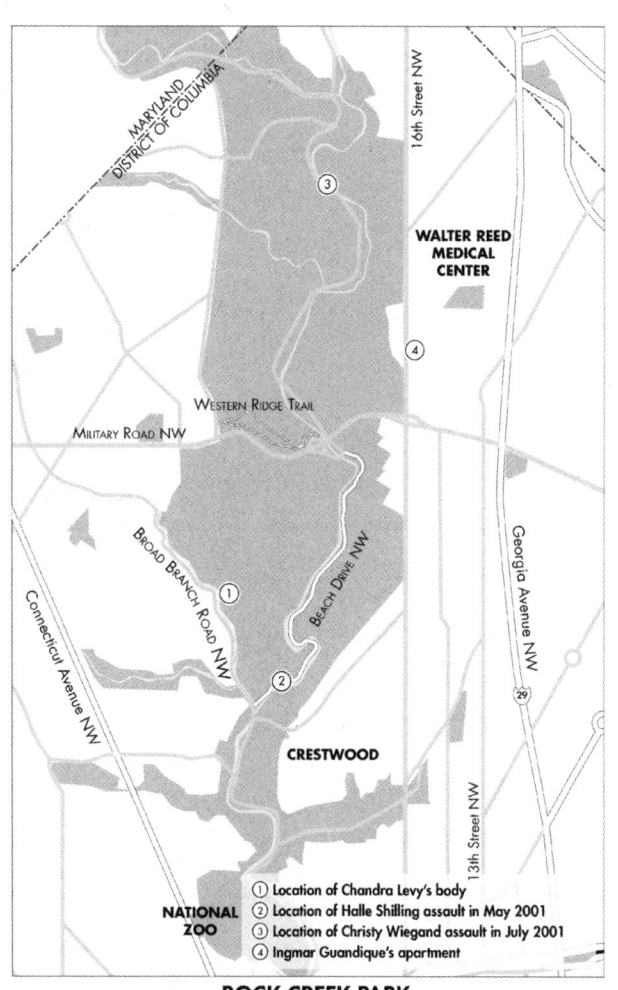

① Location of Chandra Levy's body
② Location of Halle Shilling assault in May 2001
③ Location of Christy Wiegand assault in July 2001
④ Ingmar Guandique's apartment

ROCK CREEK PARK

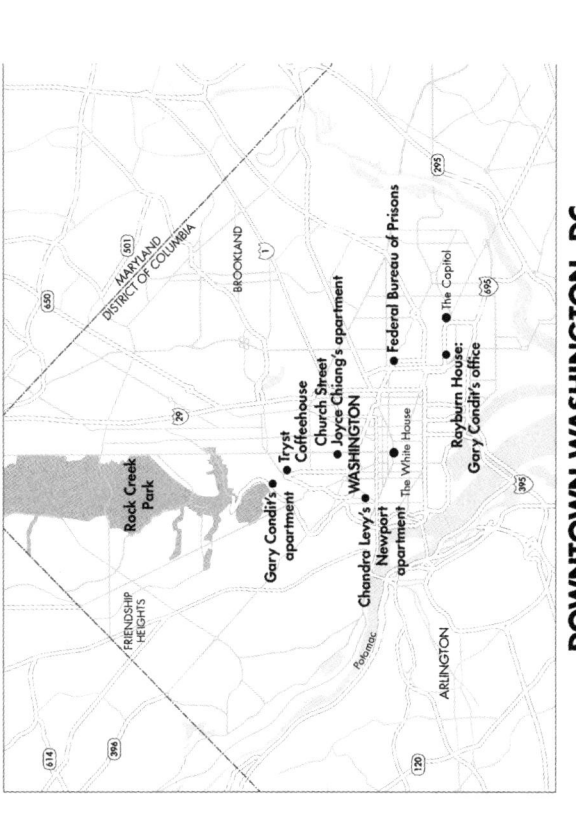

DOWNTOWN WASHINGTON, DC

Timeline

April 14, 1977: Chandra Levy is born.

September 14, 2000: Chandra Levy lands in Washington.

October 2000: The day Chandra Levy and Gary Condit (allegedly) first meet.

April 23, 2001: Chandra's internship at the Federal Bureau of Prisons comes to an abrupt end.

April 24, 2001: Chandra Levy shows up at Gary Condit's apartment. This is the last time they will see each other.

April 28, 2001: Carolyn Condit goes to Washington. Chandra Levy emails her landlord to say she will have to move out on short notice.

April 29, 2001: Gary Condit attends a luncheon at the White House to celebrate the first hundred days of George W. Bush's presidency. Chandra Levy and Gary Condit have their last phone call. Chandra leaves a message on her aunt Linda Zamsky's voicemail, saying she has "big news."

May 1, 2001: Chandra Levy's last signs of life. Gary Condit is back in the White House, where he has an appointment with Vice President Dick Cheney. Amber Fitzgerald sees a threatening man who looks like Ingmar Guandique in Rock Creek Park.

May 14, 2001: Halle Shilling is assaulted in Rock Creek Park.

July 1, 2001: Christy Wiegand is assaulted in Rock Creek Park.

July 6, 2001: Linda Zamsky describes the details of the relationship between Chandra and Gary Condit to *The Washington Post*.

Summer of 2001: The media goes into a frenzy over the Chandra Levy case.

September 11, 2001: The United States is hit by the 9/11 terrorist attacks (World Trade Center and Pentagon).

February 2, 2002: Ingmar Guandique is sentenced to ten years in prison for the two assaults in Rock Creek Park.

March 6, 2002: Gary Condit loses the election and his seat in the House of Representatives.

May 22, 2002: Chandra Levy's remains are found in Rock Creek Park.

October 25, 2010, to November 22, 2010: Ingmar Guandique is tried for the murder of Chandra Levy.

February 11, 2011: Ingmar Guandique is sentenced to sixty years in prison for the murder of Chandra Levy.

July 2015: Babs Proller meets Armando Morales in a Maryland hotel.

July 28, 2016: Charges against Ingmar Guandique are dropped.

May 8, 2017: Ingmar Guandique is deported to El Salvador.

Sources

This book is the result of months of research, drawing on books, articles, and court records, as well as several weeks of reporting during October, 2023, in Modesto, California; Washington, DC; and Maryland. It is also based on many interviews with Chandra's family and friends, as well as journalists who worked on the case, communications experts, and detectives.

Books

Daugherty, Ralph. *Murder on a Horse Trail: The Disappearance of Chandra Levy.* iUniverse Inc, 2004.

Higham, Scott and Sari Horwitz. *Finding Chandra: A True Washington Murder Mystery.* Scribner, 2011.

Peace, Breton and Gary Condit. *Actual Malice: A True Crime Political Thriller.* Ghost Mountain Books, 2016.

Wright, David, Don Gentile, Nicholas Maier. *Sex, Power & Murder: From the Files of the National Enquirer.* AMI Books, 2002.

Yarrow, Allison. *90s Bitch: Media, Culture, and the Failed Promise of Gender Equality.* HarperCollins, 2018.

Articles

I based my research on many articles, including the following: all of Michael Doyle's articles, from 2001 to 2017, published in *The Modesto Bee* or other McClatchy newspapers; *New York Post* and *National Enquirer* articles from the summer of 2001; Lisa DePaulo's article entitled "Secret and Lies" in *Talk* magazine, published in September 2001; all *Washington Post* articles on the case, and especially the "Who Killed Chandra Levy?" series, by Sari Horwitz, Scott Higham, and Sylvia Moreno, published in the summer of 2008; and other publications by CNN, *Salon*, *Newsweek*, *The Daily Beast*, the *SFGate,* and more.

Acknowledgments

I am especially grateful to Susan and Robert Levy, who took time out of their vacation—a time that should be joyful—to meet with me and dive back into a painful past so they could help me get to know Chandra. By the way, Susan and Robert, you were right: I did cross paths with a few ladybugs while working on this story. I'd like to thank Linda Zamsky, for her precious memories and frank conversations.

I couldn't have told this story without Michael Doyle's help, honesty, documents, and humor. Thanks also go out to Ralph Daugherty and Joe McCann.

To Judy Smith, Garth Stapley, and Jakub Mosur: Thanks for agreeing to enlighten me. And thank you to the authors of the books I pored over: Sari Horwitz and

Scott Higham for their irritating excellence; *National Enquirer* reporters David Wright, Don Gentile, and Nicholas Maier, wherever they are today, for the kind of information you can find only in tabloids . . . and with a touch of guilt; and Allison Yarrow, for her impressive nonfiction book about women in the nineties.

Lastly, I'd like to thank my two editors, Elsa Delachair, for trusting me, and Stéphane Régy, as always, for noticing that my usual obsessions were reflected in this story. Thanks to Olivier and to all my friends for listening to my gruesome tales of murder.

About the Author

Hélène Coutard has been an independent journalist for ten years. She writes about American literature and current events, tapping into the country's neuroses. She also covers stories related to women's rights around the world. Over the years, she has reported on the #MeToo movement, the Parkland shooting, Donald Trump's election and reelection, and the war in Ukraine. Coutard is the author of the 2021 book *Les Fugitives: Partir ou mourir en Arabie saoudite* (Fugitives: Leave or Die in Saudi Arabia), about a diaspora of young Saudi women who have fled to escape the country's male guardianship system. Her forthcoming debut novel will be published by Éditions Grasset.